Elizabeth

Fifty Glorious Years

Jennie Bond

CARLTON
BOOKS

This is a Carlton Book

This edition published by Carlton
Publishing Group 2003
20 Mortimer Street
London
W1T 3JW

A CIP catalogue for this book is
available from the British Library.

ISBN 1 84222 831 5

Executive Editor: Sarah Larter
Art Editor: Adam Wright
Design: Peter Bailey
Editorial: Janice Anderson
Production: Marianna Wolf

Printed in Dubai

Contents

Elizabeth Family Tree

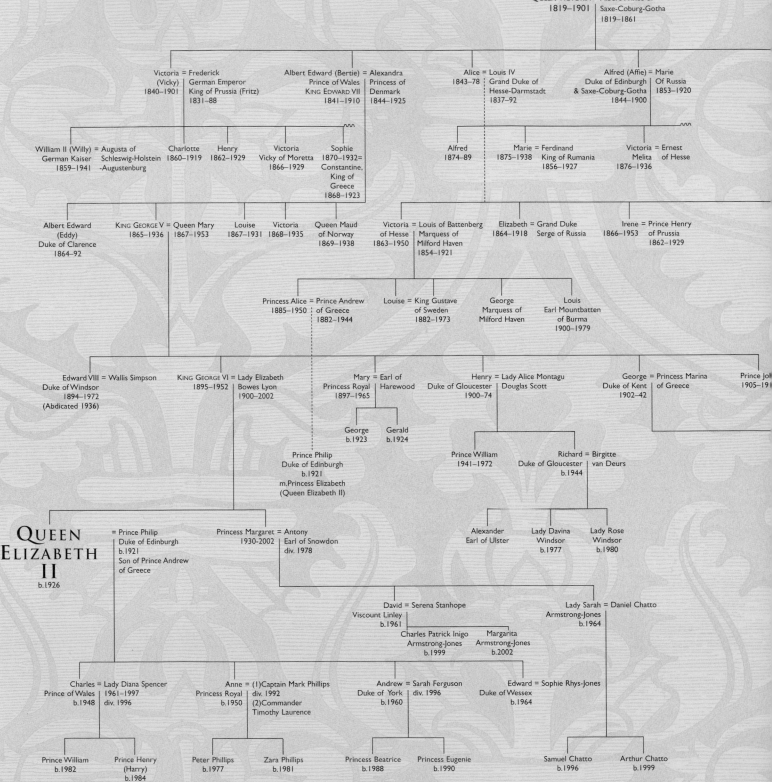

QUEEN VICTORIA = Albert Prince of
1819–1901 | Saxe-Coburg-Gotha
1819–1861

Victoria = Frederick
(Vicky) | German Emperor
1840–1901 | King of Prussia (Fritz)
1831–88

Albert Edward (Bertie) = Alexandra
Prince of Wales | Princess of
KING EDWARD VII | Denmark
1841–1910 | 1844–1925

Alice = Louis IV
1843–78 | Grand Duke of
Hesse-Darmstadt
1837–92

Alfred (Affie) = Marie
Duke of Edinburgh | Of Russia
& Saxe-Coburg-Gotha | 1853–1920
1844–1900

William II (Willy) = Augusta of
German Kaiser | Schleswig-Holstein
1859–1941 | -Augustenburg

Charlotte
1860–1919

Henry
1862–1929

Victoria
Vicky of Moretta
1866–1929

Sophie
1870–1932=
Constantine,
King of
Greece
1868–1923

Alfred
1874–89

Marie = Ferdinand
1875–1938 | King of Rumania
1856–1927

Victoria = Ernest
Melita | of Hesse
1876–1936

Albert Edward
(Eddy)
Duke of Clarence
1864–92

KING GEORGE V = Queen Mary
1865–1936 | 1867–1953

Louise
1867–1931

Victoria
1868–1935

Queen Maud
of Norway
1869–1938

Victoria = Louis of Battenberg
of Hesse | Marquess of
1863–1950 | Milford Haven
1854–1921

Elizabeth = Grand Duke
1864–1918 | Serge of Russia

Irene = Prince Henry
1866–1953 | of Prussia
1862–1929

Princess Alice = Prince Andrew
1885–1950 | of Greece
1882–1944

Louise = King Gustave
of Sweden
1882–1973

George
Marquess of
Milford Haven

Louis
Earl Mountbatten
of Burma
1900–1979

Edward VIII = Wallis Simpson
Duke of Windsor
1894–1972
(Abdicated 1936)

KING GEORGE VI = Lady Elizabeth
1895–1952 | Bowes Lyon
1900–2002

Mary = Earl of
Princess Royal | Harewood
1897–1965

Henry = Lady Alice Montagu
Duke of Gloucester | Douglas Scott
1900–74

George = Princess Marina
Duke of Kent | of Greece
1902–42

Prince Jo
1905–19

George
b.1923

Gerald
b.1924

Prince Philip
Duke of Edinburgh
b.1921
m.Princess Elizabeth
(Queen Elizabeth II)

Prince William
1941–1972

Richard = Birgitte
Duke of Gloucester | van Deurs
b.1944

QUEEN
ELIZABETH
II
b.1926

= Prince Philip
Duke of Edinburgh
b.1921
Son of Prince Andrew
of Greece

Princess Margaret = Antony
1930-2002 | Earl of Snowdon
div. 1978

Alexander
Earl of Ulster

Lady Davina
Windsor
b.1977

Lady Rose
Windsor
b.1980

David = Serena Stanhope
Viscount Linley
b.1961

Lady Sarah = Daniel Chatto
Armstrong-Jones
b.1964

Charles Patrick Inigo
Armstrong-Jones
b.1999

Margarita
Armstrong-Jones
b.2002

Charles = Lady Diana Spencer
Prince of Wales | 1961–1997
b.1948 | div. 1996

Anne = (1)Captain Mark Phillips
Princess Royal | div. 1992
b.1950 | (2)Commander
Timothy Laurence

Andrew = Sarah Ferguson
Duke of York | div. 1996
b.1960

Edward = Sophie Rhys-Jones
Duke of Wessex
b.1964

Prince William
b.1982

Prince Henry
(Harry)
b.1984

Peter Phillips
b.1977

Zara Phillips
b.1981

Princess Beatrice
b.1988

Princess Eugenie
b.1990

Samuel Chatto
b.1996

Arthur Chatto
b.1999

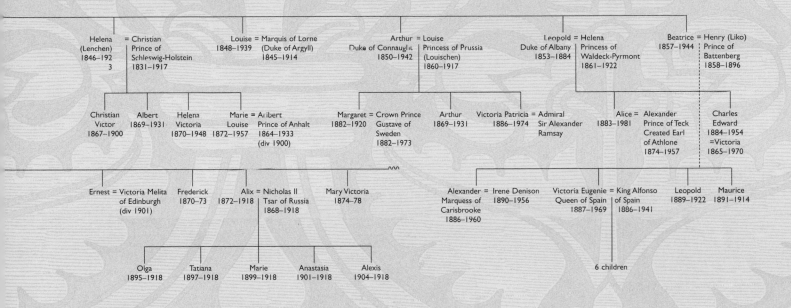

Helena (Lenchen) 1846–1923 = Christian Prince of Schleswig-Holstein 1831–1917

Louise 1848–1939 = Marquis of Lorne (Duke of Argyll) 1845–1914

Arthur Duke of Connaught 1850–1942 = Louise Princess of Prussia (Louischen) 1860–1917

Leopold Duke of Albany 1853–1884 = Helena Princess of Waldeck-Pyrmont 1861–1922

Beatrice 1857–1944 = Henry (Liko) Prince of Battenberg 1858–1896

Christian Victor 1867–1900

Albert 1869–1931

Helena Victoria 1870–1948

Marie Louise 1872–1957 = Aribert Prince of Anhalt 1864–1933 (div 1900)

Margaret 1882–1920 = Crown Prince Gustave of Sweden 1882–1973

Arthur 1869–1931

Victoria Patricia 1886–1974 = Admiral Sir Alexander Ramsay

Alice 1883–1981 = Alexander Prince of Teck Created Earl of Athlone 1874–1957

Charles Edward 1884–1954 = Victoria 1865–1970

Ernest 1870–73 = Victoria Melita of Edinburgh (div 1901)

Frederick 1870–73

Alix 1872–1918 = Nicholas II Tsar of Russia 1868–1918

Mary Victoria 1874–78

Alexander Marquess of Carisbrooke 1886–1960 = Irene Denison 1890–1956

Victoria Eugenie Queen of Spain 1887–1969 = King Alfonso of Spain 1886–1941

Leopold 1889–1922

Maurice 1891–1914

Olga 1895–1918

Tatiana 1897–1918

Marie 1899–1918

Anastasia 1901–1918

Alexis 1904–1918

6 children

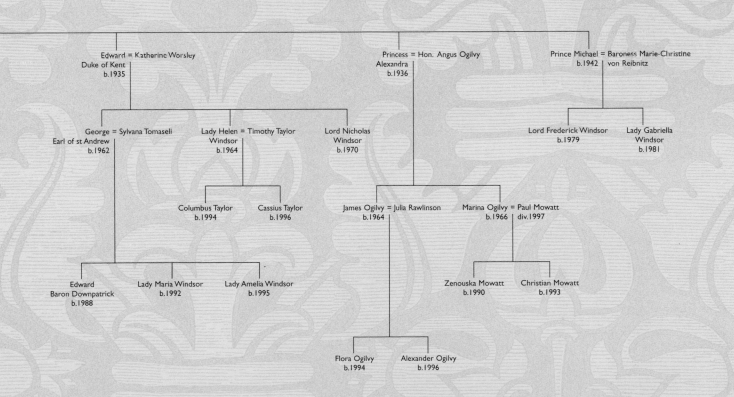

Edward Duke of Kent b.1935 = Katherine Worsley

Princess Alexandra b.1936 = Hon. Angus Ogilvy

Prince Michael b.1942 = Baroness Marie-Christine von Reibnitz

George Earl of st Andrew b.1962 = Sylvana Tomaseli

Lady Helen Windsor b.1964 = Timothy Taylor

Lord Nicholas Windsor b.1970

Lord Frederick Windsor b.1979

Lady Gabriella Windsor b.1981

Columbus Taylor b.1994

Cassius Taylor b.1996

James Ogilvy b.1964 = Julia Rawlinson

Marina Ogilvy b.1966 = Paul Mowatt div.1997

Edward Baron Downpatrick b.1988

Lady Maria Windsor b.1992

Lady Amelia Windsor b.1995

Zenouska Mowatt b.1990

Christian Mowatt b.1993

Flora Ogilvy b.1994

Alexander Ogilvy b.1996

INTRODUCTION

PRINCESS ELIZABETH

WHAT'S THE QUEEN REALLY LIKE? It's a question I've been asked more times than I care to remember during my years of reporting on royalty for the BBC. The answer to it is not simple. She is, without doubt, one of the most famous women in the world: hundreds of thousands of people have met her, scores of books have been written about her and she has even starred in a couple of television documentaries examining her life and work. I've chatted with her on numerous occasions around the world and have generally found her easy to get along with and surprisingly funny. But only an inner sanctum of a very few trusted relatives and friends can honestly claim to know the Queen. Partly by nature and partly because of the job that she holds, Elizabeth has always been a deeply private person. She's not naturally tactile, doesn't easily show her emotions and is also quite shy. Those characteristics, combined with an inevitable isolation because she is the Queen, have led some people to view her as cold and remote. Her friends believe she is misunderstood.

It is hard to think of a lonelier role than that of monarch. For fifty years the Queen has held that position, steering a careful constitutional path through a minefield of political, social and domestic crises without the luxury of a raft of colleagues in whom she can confide. She has presided over an era of profound sociological change throughout the Commonwealth and a technological revolution that has shrunk the globe. Prime Ministers and world leaders have come and gone, political maps have been re-drawn but, for half a century, the Queen has fulfilled her role as figurehead and matriarch. Her greatest achievement for many people is the very fact of her presence: providing a sense of continuity and stability in ever shifting sands.

On each day of her long reign she has ploughed through the Red Boxes that are delivered to her wherever she is, regardless of whether she is "on holiday". Inside is a mound of documents about matters of state ranging from the mundane to the mighty. All require her attention or signature and not even her husband is party to their contents. As Sovereign, she stands alone – above politics and with a job description that entitles her only to warn, encourage and be consulted by her Government. As a mother, she heads a troubled family and has endured the misery of watching the marriages of three of her children disintegrate in the glare of publicity without allowing herself to betray the merest flicker of emotion. For she believes that, as Queen, she must remain apart from the rest of us, and even those in her inner circle keep a respectful distance. Her advisers are mindful – perhaps too mindful – of her status. It is a dilemma that can spawn obfuscation, as she acknowledged publicly during the celebrations that marked her Golden Wedding Anniversary in 1997. It was only two months after the death of Diana, Princess of Wales and, at a lunch attended by the Prime Minister, the Queen spoke about the difficulties that the Royal Family encounter in reading public opinion: "Governments," she said, "can gauge support through the ballot box. For us, though, it is not always easy. The message can be obscured by deference or rhetoric. But read it we must."

Trying to read public opinion has, however, proved traumatic during a period of turmoil over the past decade that has seen the popularity of the Royal Family plummet dramatically at times. Occasionally – for example, in the days immediately after Diana's death – there has been a whiff of rebellion in the air, leaving the Queen appearing confused and hurt. But Elizabeth was brought up with a profound sense of duty, which has never wavered. She has unfailingly put her job before her personal happiness and family commitments – some would say at considerable cost to her children. Although she is, of course, cushioned against the everyday drudgery suffered by most of us, the Queen is and always has been a working mother and has undoubtedly experienced something of the conflict that goes with that role. Since her accession in 1952 she has carried out more than two hundred and fifty tours abroad, taking her away from her children sometimes for months at a time. The fact that this has long been an accepted way of life for royalty may have lessened the pain, but the Queen is not without maternal feelings and the long separations were not necessarily easy. Duty, though, has always prevailed over maternal feelings.

By nature Elizabeth is a countrywoman, happiest in a tweed skirt and headscarf walking her dogs, or in jodhpurs and hacking jacket (stubbornly minus the hat) riding one of her thoroughbreds. Even in her mid-seventies she enjoys a sedate gallop across her estates at Sandringham, Balmoral or Windsor. Perhaps because of the solitary job that became hers so suddenly when she was twenty-five, Elizabeth has always been something of a loner, content with her own company – when she can get it. But, as Queen, it is her duty to meet and greet tens of thousands of people each year. Her official life entails making polite conversation with strangers the world over. On numerous overseas tours I have watched her display due care and interest in the lives and thoughts of these strangers, even when yet another "cultural performance of song and dance" has over-run, her feet, like mine, must be aching and the temperature is soaring.

The Queen is not out-going by nature but she has learned to "work the crowds" and, although she has never quite rivalled her mother's effortless charm with onlookers and fans, she is a consummate professional. She also has a keen eye for the ridiculous, a dry sense of humour and in the privacy of her immediate circle she's a dab hand as a mimic.

When you meet her for the first time you may be struck, as I was, by her wide smile and the occasional mischievous glint in her eyes when something amuses her. Beware, though, of over-stepping the mark: a touch too much familiarity and you will find yourself frozen out. For she is, first and foremost, the guardian of a position that she regards as sacrosanct: in an increasingly cynical world, the Queen is potently aware that she is on the front line of defending the institution of monarchy.

It was not a role that was mapped out for her from birth. There was, of course, a great deal of public interest when news came through on April 21, 1926 that the Duke and Duchess of York had become the proud parents of a baby daughter. Elizabeth Alexandra Mary had been born in the early hours of the morning at 17 Bruton Street in London, the town residence of her maternal grandparents, the Earl and Countess of Strathmore. True, she was third in line to the throne – after her uncle, Edward, Prince of Wales, and her father. But few doubted that Edward would marry and have heirs of his own, distancing Elizabeth forever from becoming Queen.

She was less than a fortnight old when the country was plunged into chaos with the start of the General Strike. But after six difficult days, order was restored and the plans went ahead for Elizabeth's christening. It took place in the private chapel at Buckingham Palace on May 29.

When the family moved to a new, spacious home at 145 Piccadilly the baby and her nanny, Clara Knight (universally known as Allah), were allocated the top floor of the house. It was Allah's face that the young Elizabeth came to know best as her parents pursued the lifestyle of most aristocrats at that time, leaving the nitty-gritty of baby care to their staff. Royal duties also impinged on their time with their daughter. In January 1927, when Elizabeth was nine months old, the Duke and Duchess set off on a six-month tour to Panama, Fiji, Australia and New Zealand. Their child, meanwhile, spent her first birthday with her grandparents, George V and Queen Mary, at Windsor Castle.

The other key figures in the young Elizabeth's life were her sister, Margaret Rose, who arrived on the scene in 1930, and their governess Marion Crawford, or "Crawfie", who took up her post three years later. Her appointment effectively completed the Princess's isolation from the world beyond royal circles. Neither of the girls would ever know what it was like to be part of a school community. It's strange to think that during the hundreds of visits to schools and colleges that Elizabeth has subsequently made, she has never been able to identify personally with the experiences of the children she sees. Although Crawfie did her best to take the young Princesses on educational visits outside the Palace – sometimes even by tube – the classroom must have been a lonely place for them, with no other children to share their lessons. The closest they got to "mucking in" with the crowd was in the select Girl Guide Company that was eventually set up at the Palace.

By all accounts, though, they enjoyed a contented family life with their parents. The Duke of York was a doting father who was not over-burdened by his workload. They divided their time between their London home and Royal Lodge in Windsor Great Park, which had been given to the Duke and Duchess by George V when Elizabeth was four. They had horses and dogs and a life of privilege without

great responsibility. It was a period of intense happiness and security for them all. Before long, however, everything would change.

George V was already ailing in July 1935 as the country celebrated the Silver Jubilee of his accession. Six months later, he died at Sandringham, with his wife and children at his bedside. His eldest son, David, was proclaimed King and took the title Edward VIII. Elizabeth moved one step nearer to the throne.

Still, though, the expectation remained that the new King would find a wife and produce an heir. But that was without bargaining for the irresistible pull of Wallis Simpson – American, twice-divorced and utterly bewitching to David. Forced to choose between her and the throne, he followed his heart – and Elizabeth's fate was sealed. She was ten years old and the Heir Presumptive.

Edward VIII's Abdication in December 1936 altered her life forever, though the full repercussions may not have sunk in immediately. Years later, Princess Margaret recalled her sister's reaction to this sudden change of destiny: "When our father became King, I said to her, 'Does that mean you're going to be Queen?' She replied, 'Yes, I suppose it does.' She didn't mention it again."

Reluctantly, for neither George VI nor Queen Elizabeth had wanted their new roles, the family moved to Buckingham Palace. They had a tough job ahead: to restore the public's faith in the monarchy. In pursuit of that, they relied heavily on the harmonious image projected by their tight-knit unit. Pictures of "we four", as the King described his family, provided reassurance in the aftermath of the Abdication and in the menacing years leading up to the outbreak of the Second World War.

Elizabeth and Margaret spent those war years quietly at Windsor, often retreating to the dungeons beneath the Castle as the Luftwaffe screamed overhead. Although the two sisters were very different in character: Elizabeth rather serious and responsible, Margaret extrovert and naughty, this enforced exile brought them close as children. They dabbled at putting on their own entertainment for specially invited guests, staging regular concerts and Christmas pantomimes in the Castle's Waterloo Chamber.

But Elizabeth was keen to play her part in the war effort and, in 1945, she finally persuaded her parents to allow her to join the Auxiliary Territorial Service. It was only a few months before the war in Europe ended but, for a time at least, the Princess learned a little of life as the rest of us know it. She was taught how to strip an engine, change a wheel and drive an army truck. She wore her uniform proudly on VE Day when, for an hour or so, she seized another brief but graphic glimpse of the world outside her ivory tower. As she stood on the balcony of Buckingham Palace with her mother and father acknowledging the cheers of the crowds below, Elizabeth wanted only one thing – to be able to join in their celebrations. In a rare interview, recorded many years afterwards, she described what happened:

> My mother had put her tiara on for the occasion, so we asked my parents if we could go out and see for ourselves. I remember we were terrified of being recognized so I pulled my uniform cap well down over my eyes. A Grenadier officer amongst our party of about sixteen people said he refused to be seen in the company of another officer improperly dressed. So I had to put my cap on normally. We cheered the King and Queen on the balcony and then walked miles through the streets. I remember lines of unknown people linking arms and walking down Whitehall, all of us just swept along on a tide of happiness and relief.

Anonymous and one of the crowd: it was a unique treat for the Princesses and gave them a taste of freedom that they must have relished.

The end of the war also brought the return home of a serviceman who had already won Elizabeth's heart – though few knew it then. Lieutenant Prince Philip of Greece, tall, blue-eyed and blonde was something of an Adonis, and by all accounts the Princess had been smitten by him since she was thirteen. Though their paths had crossed at various family functions (they are third cousins) it was a meeting at the Royal Naval College at Dartmouth in 1939 that sowed the seeds of their subsequent romance. It was shortly before the outbreak of war, and the King and Queen and their daughters sailed into Dartmouth on an official visit. Philip, then a handsome eighteen-year-old Cadet Captain, was assigned to look after the girls. Elizabeth was bowled over.

"She never took her eyes off him," wrote her governess, Crawfie, in her memoirs. "At the tennis courts I thought he showed off a good deal, but the little girls were much impressed."

Elizabeth, though, was scarcely more than a child; and Philip was about to go to war. There were occasional letters between them during those years of conflict, and Philip was invited to spend Christmas at Windsor in 1943. But it was only in 1946, when he returned from service in the Far East, that the rumours of romance began to take hold. Elizabeth was now twenty and, it seems, sure of her feelings. The King, though, was less positive; he thought she was too young to marry and should have the opportunity to meet other potential husbands. He and the Queen counselled their daughter to take her time – and in February 1947 whisked her off on a four-month tour of South Africa.

It was there that Princess Elizabeth made one of her most historic broadcasts, dedicating her life to the service of the Empire and Commonwealth. The occasion was her twenty first birthday; the venue Cape Town. In a clear, high-pitched voice she said:

> I declare before you that my whole life, whether it be long or short, shall be devoted to your service and the service of our great Imperial family to which we all belong. But I shall not have the strength to carry out this resolution alone unless you join in with me, as I now invite you to do. I know that your support will be unfailingly given. God help me to make good my vow and God bless all of you who are willing to share in it.

A few days later, the Royal Family set sail for home. It soon became obvious that the enforced separation had done nothing to cool Elizabeth and Philip's ardour and, shortly after her return, their engagement was announced. The wedding was to be on November 20, 1947 in the grand setting of Westminster Abbey. It turned out to be a cold, blustery morning, but thousands of people lined the streets from Buckingham Palace to the Abbey, cheering as the young bride passed by in the Irish State Coach. For a day at least, the austerity of the postwar years was obscured. In a letter to his daughter afterwards, the King wistfully acknowledged that the wedding had signalled the end of an era, he wrote

> I was so proud of you and thrilled at having you so close to me on our long walk in Westminster Abbey. But when I handed your hand to the Archbishop I felt I had lost something very precious. You were so calm and composed during the Service and said your words with such conviction that I knew everything was all right.

Elizabeth was undoubtedly very much in love with her man. He may have been virtually penniless, but his good looks made him quite a head turner and his blood was as royal as her own. The son of a Greek Prince, he was also a direct descendant of Queen Victoria and had strong links with the Danish royal family and, even more so, with Germany. Those links – graphically illustrated when all four of his sisters married Germans – were an obvious embarrassment in the postwar climate, and Philip swiftly became a British national with the surname Mountbatten. Even as a young man, he was fiercely independent; he found the strictures on his new life irksome. The situation wasn't helped by the fact that their marital home, Clarence House, wasn't ready – leaving them living at Buckingham Palace with the in-laws.

Within a year, though, Elizabeth and Philip were parents themselves. Charles Philip Arthur George was born on the evening of November 14, 1948. The crowds who gathered outside the Palace cheered until well after midnight. Sadly, alongside the joy of new motherhood, Elizabeth had the worry of her father's increasing frailty; he was only in his fifties, but his health was failing. Two days after his grandson's birth he was forced to postpone a trip to Australia and New Zealand.

Summer 1949 saw Elizabeth and Philip finally move in to Clarence House. They relished the independence it brought them but there was little chance to settle down as a family unit as Philip's naval career took him to Malta. Over the next two years, the Princess spent long periods with her husband on the island, enjoying life as a navy wife. She was freer than she would ever be again and she loved it. Charles, meanwhile, was looked after by nannies and grandparents – a fact that did not appear to trouble her unduly. After one absence of some five weeks, she returned to Clarence House to catch up with correspondence for four days before being reunited with Charles, who was at Sandringham. Soon, though, her family expanded: in August 1950, she gave birth to her second child, Anne.

As the King's health declined, more and more duties devolved to the Princess. In 1951, Philip accepted that he could no longer combine his naval career with his royal role and returned from Malta to support his wife. Before long she needed that support urgently.

The precise moment of Elizabeth's accession to the throne will never be known, but it was some time in the early hours of February 6, 1952. She and Philip were staying in the original Treetops Hotel, perched high in a wild fig tree in Kenya. They were en route to Australia and New Zealand, representing the King who was now suffering from cancer. At Sandringham meanwhile, despite his frailty George VI had enjoyed a day's shooting before sitting down to dinner with his wife and Princess Margaret. He seemed relaxed and listened to the latest radio reports about Elizabeth's progress in Africa before going to bed at about 10.30pm. That night he died in his sleep. At the instant of his death, the throne passed to Elizabeth.

May 1926: one month old and all dressed up for her christening, Princess Elizabeth is watched over by her mother, the Duchess of York. The Princess's satin robe trimmed with Honiton lace was made for Queen Victoria's children. Tradition dictates that it is the dress still used for royal christenings.

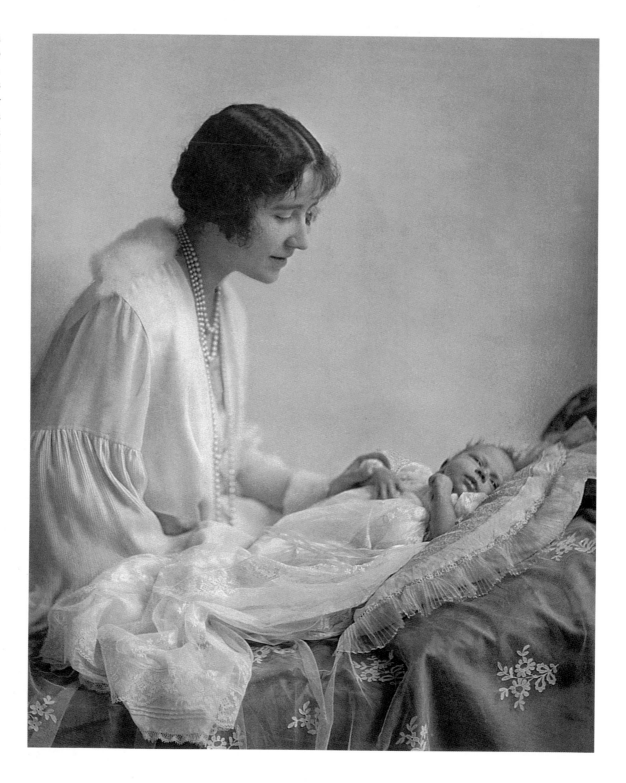

1932 – immaculately dressed for a spot of bucket-and-spade work, Elizabeth, aged six and two-year-old Margaret prepare to get their hands dirty.

May 12, 1937, King George VI's Coronation Day. Elizabeth stands on the Buckingham Palace balcony with her newly crowned parents, her sister and her grandmother, Queen Mary. In her diary that night, eleven-year-old Elizabeth wrote: "I thought it all very, very wonderful and I expect the Abbey did, too. The arches and beams at the top were covered with a sort of haze of wonder as Papa was crowned, at least I thought so."

Looking rather tickled by an impressive
feather, the Princesses chat with an officer
of the Royal Company of Archers. With their
parents they were attending a function in
the grounds of Holyroodhouse Palace: the
sovereign's official residence in Scotland.

Peaceful days at Royal Lodge, Windsor.
The two sisters tackle their knitting (their
father was a prodigious knitter) as the
dogs look on. Both Princesses knitted socks
for servicemen during the Second World War.

This photograph, taken in 1942, shows Elizabeth wearing a hat with a distinctly military style, in keeping with the fashions of wartime Britain. She longed to play a part in the war effort but, on her sixteenth birthday, she had to content herself with an honorary role as Colonel of the Grenadier Guards.

Another wartime morale-boosting picture, this photograph shows the Princess working on the royal farm at Sandringham, Norfolk in 1944. Always at home with animals, Elizabeth, aged eighteen, windblown and carefree, leads one of the farm horses during the harvest.

Off-duty during their long South African tour,
Elizabeth and Margaret let off some steam
cantering along a beach in March, 1947.

Who says she's repressed and formal? Elizabeth joins in the fun of deck games on board HMS *Vanguard,* the ship that took the Royal Family to South Africa in 1947. George VI hoped that the tour would take his young daughter's mind off her love affair with Philip but, after four months apart, her heart was still set on him.

November 20, 1947, and Elizabeth is married at last! Despite last-minute crises – her tiara snapped and then her bouquet went missing – Elizabeth made it to Westminster Abbey to marry her man. Her gown and 15-foot (4½-metre) train were designed by Norman Hartnell.

July 31, 1949. A rare chance to be "one of the crowd". Elizabeth and Philip sit with their close friends Lord and Lady Brabourne (Patricia Mountbatten, daughter of Philip's uncle, Lord Mountbatten) at a village cricket match in Kent. Philip waits to bat for the local side … they won!

THE NEW QUEEN

IT TOOK MORE THAN four hours for news of the King's death to filter through to Africa. By then Elizabeth and Philip had returned to Sagana Lodge, a farm near Nairobi that had been given to them as a wedding present by the Kenyan Government. Philip took her into the garden and walked with her slowly as they absorbed the full implications of what had happened. Far from home and aged just twenty-five Elizabeth had not only lost her much-loved father but also any vestige of carefree youth. She was now Queen and Head of State.

Her first decision was how she would be known. Her private secretary asked quietly what she wanted to be called: "My own name, Elizabeth," she replied as she sat upright at her desk, accepting her destiny. Another in the royal party recollects that "her feelings were deep, deep inside her."

A few hours later, they were on their way home to a solemn greeting at the airport from her Prime Minister, Winston Churchill, the leader of the Opposition, Clement Attlee and the Foreign Secretary, Anthony Eden. Dressed in black and looking pale, the new Queen told Churchill, "This is a very tragic homecoming."

Though she no doubt wanted to be at her mother's side, Elizabeth had first to attend a full meeting of the Accession Council. It took place the next day in the white and gold Throne Room at St James's Palace. There she made her Declaration of Accession. She spoke both as monarch and grieving daughter:

By the sudden death of my dear father, I am called to assume the duties and responsibility of Sovereignty … My father was our revered and beloved head as he was of the wider family of his subjects. The grief which his loss brings is shared among us all … I pray that God will help me to discharge worthily this heavy task that has been laid upon me so early in my life.

She then drove to Sandringham to be with her mother who, at the age of fifty-one, had lost both her husband and her role. In a message to the world the Queen Mother, as she now was, spoke of her sadness:

Your concern for me has upheld me in my sorrow and how proud you have made me by your wonderful tributes to my dear husband, a great and noble King.

I commend to you our dear daughter: give her your loyalty and devotion in the great and lonely station to which she has been called. She will need your protection and love.

On February 11, the coffin bearing the King's body was brought from Sandringham to lie in state in Westminster Hall. Over the next three days, 305,806 people filed past to say their farewells to a King who had taken on his role so reluctantly but had seen the country through some of its darkest days. The funeral was held on February 15. The new Queen sprinkled earth on her father's coffin as it was lowered into the royal vaults at St George's Chapel in Windsor. She cut a lonely figure – now embarked on her peculiarly solitary destiny.

The novelty of having a woman on the throne and, in this case, a youthful and rather pretty one, set Fleet Street on fire. She was dubbed the "fairytale Queen" and "the hope of our nation"; she learned quickly that wherever she went, cameras would follow. The royal story was big news – and now it had a glamorous heroine to help it along. In June, she took the salute at the Trooping the Colour; in November she donned crown and jewels for the carriage procession to the State Opening of Parliament; and in December she made her first Christmas broadcast. Meanwhile her children, Charles and Anne, adapted to their new surroundings at Buckingham Palace, and became used to their mother being busier than ever. Like other mothers of her background, the Queen was content to leave the bulk of the business of child rearing to nannies. But she was always keen to spend time with Charles and Anne in the early evenings and, with that in mind, she moved her weekly audience with the Prime Minister back by an hour so that she could be with the children at bath-time.

A monarch has few mentors with close experience of the pressures of the job, and a year into her reign, the Queen lost one of that elite group: her grandmother, Queen Mary. In fact, the old Dowager Queen had always been a rather stern and distant figure in Elizabeth's life. She had hoped to witness her granddaughter taking on the mantle of monarchy at her Coronation, but, with just nine weeks to go, and as final preparations for the ceremony got underway, Queen Mary died on March 24, 1953. Aware that an extended period of court mourning could disrupt all the plans, she had made it plain before her death that she wanted the Coronation to go ahead regardless. Her wish was respected and on June 2, the scene was finally set for a spectacle that would be enjoyed by hundreds of thousands of people along the coronation route – and, for the first time, by millions more who were watching television.

The decision to allow cameras into Westminster Abbey had been hard fought. The BBC and newspapers had lobbied vehemently for more public access to this national event. One columnist in the *Sunday Express* lambasted "the tight-knit group of palace officials whose determination to keep people as far as possible away from the throne never diminishes. What a bunch of codheads to run the Queen's business."

Looking back on remarks like this, made almost forty years before I began waging my own battles with the Palace, I can't resist a chuckle. It certainly proves just how slowly the wheels of change roll where royalty is concerned.

It was the Queen herself who had put up the initial objections to the filming of the Coronation. She had been supported by the Prime Minister, the Archbishop of Canterbury and the Abbey clergy, who were unanimous in their view that television would detract from the dignity of the occasion. In the end, the avalanche of protest made its mark, and the Queen changed her mind. Viewers across the country, and soon across the world, watched a ceremony unrivalled in its splendour and symbolism.

From the moment the Queen stepped into the Gold State Coach, drawn by eight Windsor greys, to their return to the Palace almost six-and-a-half hours later, the pageantry ran like clockwork and provided images of an unparalleled richness. It was the start of the television age of royal reporting; the public lapped it up. However, it was also the end of an era for the Royal Family. Eventually, they, too, would become seduced by the television cameras and some would choose to bare their souls before them.

4p.m, February 7, 1952, Heathrow Airport, London. Elizabeth had left Britain as a Princess with her father waving farewell from the tarmac. She returned as Queen to mourn his death. From the aircraft window, one of her entourage watches a moment in history as Winston Churchill and other senior politicians wait, bare-headed, to greet their new Queen.

Sisters united in sorrow as, heavily veiled, they follow their father's coffin on the first stage of its journey from Sandringham to London.

The grief of three Queens: Elizabeth, Queen Mary and Queen Elizabeth the
Queen Mother stand at the entrance to Westminster Hall as the King's coffin
is carried past them for the lying-in-state. Princess Margaret is on the right.

November 3rd 1952. Happier times as, in diamonds and pearls, the Queen sets off for her first State Opening of Parliament.

Elizabeth plays with her two children at Balmoral in September 1952. Perched precariously, three-year-old Charles looks on as Anne, aged two, seems intent on making an unorthodox entry in to her mother's sitting room.

Another picture from Balmoral in September 1952. Always keen on taking her own family snaps, the Queen tackles a complicated-looking piece of equipment while Charles, clearly fascinated, pays close attention.

The nursing staff at Great Ormond Street Hospital for Sick Children in London take a few minutes off work to welcome the new Queen, on a visit in 1952.

You're never too young for a party! With Coronation Day celebrations planned around the country in 1953, the Government announced special food concessions for street parties. In spite of the postwar rationing that still lingered on in Britain, everyone could have an extra pound (500 grams) of sugar and 4 ounces (125 grams) of margarine or cooking fat.

June 1, 1953. Anyone for a cup of tea? On the eve of the Coronation, half-a-million people camped outside Buckingham Palace and along the route of the procession, despite pouring rain and driving wind.

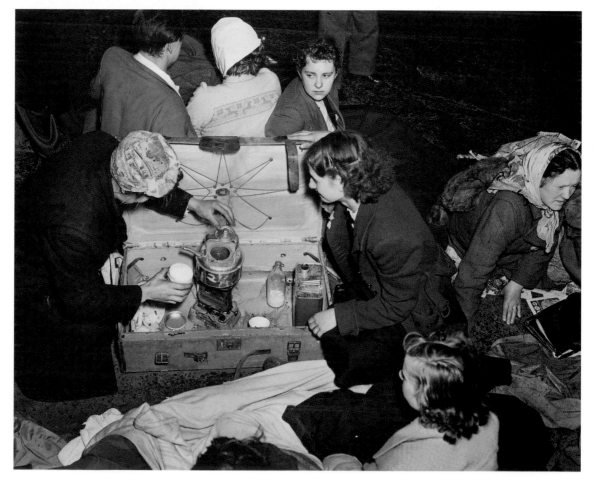

Flanked by the Bishop of Durham (on her right) and the Bishop of Bath and Wells, the Queen, in her coronation robes and with St Edward's Crown on her head, prepares to accept the homage of her Peers.

June 2, 1953, Coronation Day, and the Gold State Coach, with its ornate palm tree pillars, takes Elizabeth to Westminster Abbey. Prince Philip is at her side. The Queen is wearing one of her favourite pieces of crown jewellery, the George IV State Diadem.

Even in the drizzle, the procession back to the Palace was a stunning sight. Here, the crowds gather in Trafalgar Square to get a close-up view. That night, in a broadcast to the Commonwealth, the Queen looked back on an historic day: "As it draws to a close, I know my abiding memory will be not only the solemnity and beauty of the ceremony but the inspiration of your loyalty and affection," she said.

Most of the Royal Family were gathered together for this
Coronation photograph in the Throne Room at Buckingham
Palace. The Queen is in the centre of the group, her mother at her
side, her sister and husband behind her and her children, Charles
and Anne, in front. Others in the front row include, from left, Princess
Alice, Countess of Athlone (her robe over her left arm), Princess
Alexandra and Prince Michael of Kent and their mother, the Duchess
of Kent, the Princess Royal (to the Queen Mother's left), then the
Duchess of Gloucester with her two sons, William and Richard.

THE FIRST DECADE

1952–1961

THIS WAS THE NEW Elizabethan age. The shock of the Abdication was history, the horrors of war were fading and a good-looking young Queen had been crowned. But the Coronation had uncovered a secret that was about to rock the Royal Family again.

It was revealed in a fleeting moment away from the main focus of the ceremony. In the annexe of Westminster Abbey, a reporter had spotted Princess Margaret casually brushing a piece of fluff from the uniform of her father's former equerry, Group Captain Peter Townsend. It was a simple action that confirmed the rumours that had until then been unspoken. The Princess was in love with one of the staff – and a divorced one at that.

Fifty years on, the prospect of a Princess falling in love with a divorced man is hardly seismic. But in 1953, the Church of England, of which the Queen is head, was implacably opposed to divorce. There was also the matter of the Royal Marriages Act, which meant that, until she was twenty-five, Margaret would lose her royal status if she married without the Queen's permission. A national debate began about whether she should be allowed to follow her heart and marry Peter Townsend. To help her make up her mind, he was abruptly posted to Brussels while she was on a tour of Africa with her mother. Poll after poll found that most people thought the couple should be allowed to marry. But the establishment was unbending and, whatever the Queen's sympathy for her sister, she was unable to back her.

On October 31, 1955 Princess Margaret told the world that she had renounced her love. In a statement released that day, she said

> Mindful of the Church's teaching that Christian marriage is indissoluble, and conscious of my duty to the Commonwealth, I have resolved to put these considerations before any others. I have reached this decision entirely alone, and in doing so I have been strengthened by the unfailing support and devotion of Group Captain Townsend.

Ironically, Princess Margaret's eventual fate was to be divorced herself. Nearly forty years after her decision she was also to see her niece, Anne, end her own marriage and, with the family's blessing, marry a former palace equerry, Commander Tim Laurence. The injustice did not escape her.

For the Queen, there was little time to indulge her sister or her own family. Five months after the Coronation, she and Prince Philip set off on a six-month tour of the Commonwealth. They travelled to the Caribbean and Fiji, to Tonga and the Coco Islands and onwards to Australia and New Zealand, where they spent three months. The Queen's 1953 Christmas broadcast came from Auckland. Elizabeth was the first reigning monarch to venture so far afield, and the welcome in Sydney was effusive: "A gracious royal lady today held this city of 1,600,000 people in the hollow of her hand," gushed the evening paper. "By a ready smile she showed she was far from indifferent to all this fuss."

London's *Evening Standard* waxed equally lyrical when, in early May, the Queen and Duke arrived home, sailing up the Thames on board their new royal yacht, *Britannia*.

The fields and orchards of Kent, shaded in the bright greens of spring ... offered a soft English welcome after the sun-baked territories the Queen has trodden in recent weeks ... The Thames and the flat Essex foreshore wore an unexpected loveliness as the sun rose over them.

There is no record of the effect this prolonged parental absence had on Elizabeth and Philip's two young children.

In the spring of 1955, the Queen was called upon to use the royal prerogative for the first time. Winston Churchill finally announced his resignation, and it was her duty to appoint his successor. In many ways the choice was a foregone conclusion, though there had been a fair bit of in-fighting among Tory hopefuls. The Queen's decision to appoint Sir Anthony Eden as the new Prime Minister was executed swiftly and the transition was smooth.

The following year, 1956, saw the Queen confronted by two crises, one diplomatic and the

other domestic. In July, Egypt's President, Colonel Gamal Abdel Nasser provoked uproar by seizing the Suez Canal and nationalizing the Anglo-French company that operated it. British, French and Israeli troops went into action in October, and British bombing of Egyptian airfields, despite no declaration of war, was heavily criticized. It was a worrying time for Queen and country, not helped by the fact that international pressure soon forced a humiliating ceasefire on the three invaders. Within six months, the Queen had to appoint a new prime minister once again, Anthony Eden having resigned on the grounds of ill-health.

At home, the royal marriage had hit rocky times. Philip was frustrated by his role – or lack of one – and by the obstacles to his modernization plans that seemed constantly to be put up by old-guard courtiers. He yearned for space and freedom. When an invitation came for him to open the 1956 Olympic Games in Melbourne, he accepted eagerly. He made the most of the opportunity, setting off on a round-the-world trip on *Britannia* that would take him away from home for almost five months.

The cost of the trip – put at £1.8 million – and the Duke's absence from home at a time of national crisis played badly in the press. For a time at least, only the American papers dared to air the rumours of a marital rift. But these were given added weight when the Duke's private secretary, Mike Parker, suddenly resigned. His wife had informed the Palace that she was suing him for divorce on the grounds of adultery. Parker and the Duke – old friends from their Navy days – had certainly enjoyed themselves around the world and now there were suspicions that if Parker's marriage was over, the royal relationship could be in serious trouble too. Eventually, the Palace decided to deny the rumours, thus giving the British papers a great opportunity to print all the stories they had thus far ignored. The rumours hurt the Queen. "Why are they saying such cruel things about us?" she

asked a member of her household. She had no choice but to continue her duties. In February these took her to Portugal on a state visit, where she was reunited with her husband. Philip appeared wearing a tie covered in tiny hearts. The time out appeared to have settled him down and the Queen responded by making him a Prince of the United Kingdom. His title now was Prince Philip, Duke of Edinburgh.

The rumours of a rift may have hurt, but worse was to come. Later in 1957 an unremarkable magazine, the *National and English Review*, published a remarkable edition devoted to "The Monarchy Today." In it, the editor, Lord Altrincham, complained that the Queen's entourage were too "tweedy" and that she and Margaret were too much like debutantes. He urged her to be aware that once she had "lost the bloom of youth" she would have to say and do things that would make people take notice. And there was some blunt criticism of her speaking style. It was, he wrote

a pain in the neck … Like her mother, she appears to be unable to string even a few sentences together without a written text … The personality conveyed by the utterances which are put into her mouth is that of a priggish schoolgirl, captain of the hockey team, a prefect and a recent candidate for Confirmation.

These complaints went largely unheeded. Fifty years on the Queen still reads her speeches – no matter how short or how personal – from a script usually prepared for her by her staff.

As the first decade of Elizabeth's reign drew to a close, there were two significant family events. On February 19, 1960 the rumours of a marriage rift were finally quashed when the Queen gave birth to her third child, Prince Andrew. And in May, Princess Margaret married Anthony Armstrong-Jones, a photographer. For a time, at least, it seemed that the royal family had found unity and happiness again.

Offering comfort where she can, the Queen she sees some of the damage caused by widespread and devastating flooding in Essex and Kent in early 1953.

The Royal Tour of 1953–54 took the Queen and Prince Philip to many parts of the Pacific. Here, in Tonga, Elizabeth and Philip brace themselves for another bout of Tongan hospitality. Sitting between the Queen and Prince Philip is Queen Salote of Tonga; her broad smile as she drove in an open carriage in the pouring rain to Westminster Abbey for the Coronation, had made her one of the stars of the day. The feast she set before her royal guests in Tonga included suckling pigs, lobsters, water melons and turkeys … and those were just for starters.

Elizabeth and Philip on the New Zealand leg of their tour, in February 1954.
They were given a huge welcome in every one of the twenty towns and cities
they visited. The schedule was relentless - and the Queen's weight dropped
to below eight stone (50 kilograms). During the tour, she opened sessions of
parliament in seven countries wearing her heavy Coronation gown at each.
It has been estimated that she made 157 speeches, attended 223 balls,
receptions, garden parties and sports meetings, and shook 13,000 hands.

The Queen shows her respect for Winston Churchill by attending a Downing Street dinner to mark his retirement in April 1955. Both wear the ribbon and insignia of the Order of the Garter, Britain's grandest order of chivalry. During the evening Churchill described her as "the young, gleaming champion of a wise and kindly way of life."

Summer, 1955, and the Queen joins in the traditional pastime between games at a polo tournament: pushing back the divots cut by the hooves of the ponies. Prince Philip was an enthusiastic polo player and the Queen watched most of his matches at the ground in Windsor Great Park.

The Royal Family – and one of their many dogs – at Balmoral, in 1955. There were probably more opportunities for the Queen and Prince Philip to spend time with their children at Balmoral than anywhere else. The extensive estate on the banks of the River Dee is one of the Queen's favourite places, as it was with her great-great-grandmother, Queen Victoria.

Elizabeth and Philip re-united in Portugal in February 1957 after several months apart. After rumours of a rift in their marriage, they are back together – and the press soon note that he's wearing his heart on his tie! He had been away for almost four months; the photos were designed to quash the stories that Philip was fed up with his royal life.

The Queen meets a Hollywood legend, Marilyn Monroe, at a Royal Command Film Performance in London in October, 1956. Beside Marilyn is another Hollywood great, Victor Mature. Monroe was in London (with her then husband, playwright Arthur Miller) to make a film, *The Prince and the Showgirl*, with Laurence Olivier.

For many years, an
annual engagement in
the Royal Family's diary
was the Badminton
Horse Trials, held in the
grounds of the Duke of
Beaufort's country estate
in Gloucestershire.
In April 1957, the crowd
was given a ringside
view of the Queen, her
sister and mother sitting
on the grass near one
of the many formidable
obstacles on the
cross-country course.
Elizabeth concentrates
on her camerawork,
while Margaret
savours a cigarette.

The Queen spends most her life being chauffeured around
but, whenever she can, she seizes the chance to drive herself.
Here, Charles and Anne are her passengers at Windsor in 1957.

In October, 1957 the Queen and Prince Philip visited the United States for the three-hundred-and-fiftieth anniversary of the founding of Virginia Colony. Here, they are shown the view from the top of the Empire State Building in New York. More than half-a-million Americans turned out to see her and she was hailed the "Belle of New York".

At the first night of the hugely successful musical, *My Fair Lady*, in London in May, 1958, the Queen talks to the stars of the show – Rex Harrison, Julie Andrews and Stanley Holloway.

Not her normal stamping ground, nor her usual royal visit attire; the Queen makes her first trip down a coal mine at Rothes Colliery in Thornton, Fifeshire, in July 1958. She spent forty minutes underground, bent double at times as she crept towards the coal face.

October 1958: showing off her hour-glass figure, the Queen makes her way to the throne in the House of Lords for the State Opening of Parliament in October 1958.

Smiles all round as new technology
beckons. Watched by Prince Philip
and the Postmaster General, Ernest Marples,
the Queen inaugurates the Trunk Dialing
Service at Bristol in December 1958.
Bristol exchange was the first in Britain
to have STD facilities and the Queen marked
the occasion by calling all the way to
Edinburgh for a chat with the Lord Provost.

The Queen and nine-year-old Princess Anne messing
about with a boat – in their riding gear. Mother
and daughter are both skilled riders and have always
shared a passion for horses and the outdoor life.

The Queen appears transfixed by two of Hollywood's most famous
assets of the time: Jayne Mansfield's breasts. The star was presented
to the Queen at the 1959 Royal Command Film Performance.
The film was *Will Success Spoil Rock Hunter?*

A French state visit to
London, April 1960.
Queen and country
set out to impress
the French President,
General Charles de
Gaulle, in the hope
that he would drop his
opposition to Britain's
entry into the Common
Market. It didn't work.

Princess Margaret, newly married to Anthony Armstrong-Jones, curtsies to her sister and sovereign after the marriage ceremony in Westminster Abbey on May 5, 1960. The match, though regarded as a curious one at the time, was a relief to Elizabeth who believed that Margaret had at last found life-long happiness.

1960 February, and a new Prince is born. A couple of months before her thirty-fourth birthday, the Queen gave birth to her second son, Andrew. Why the ten-year gap between babies? Most people put it down to the fact that she had found her new job as monarch incredibly demanding. Now, after eight years of experience, she was feeling less pressured. Prince Philip's reluctance to have more children may also have had something to do with it.

A tiger hunt in Jaipur was seen by many as the low point of an otherwise successful tour of the Indian sub-continent in 1961 that sparked memories of the British Raj. This photograph of Prince Philip, his wife and friends gathered round the corpse of a tiger he had just shot provoked a chorus of outrage when it was published on almost every front page in London the next day. Philip never shot another one and has since worked to save the Indian tiger from extinction.

Drinking in the beauty of the Taj Mahal during the Indian tour. The Queen, who was the first British monarch to visit India since her grandfather, George V half a century earlier, was welcomed by a vast crowd of more than a million people.

Elizabeth photographed at Ahmedabad during the tour of India. Despite the sun and the heat she seldom appeared in a large-brimmed hat, because, as she often said, "people want to see me".

At first glance it may look like New York but this was Karachi in Pakistan, where the Queen was driven through the streets in a gleaming cream Cadillac.

Over the years the Queen has grown used to being presented with a bizarre assortment of gifts during her travels. This time it's a goat, offered during the 1961 visit to Pakistan.

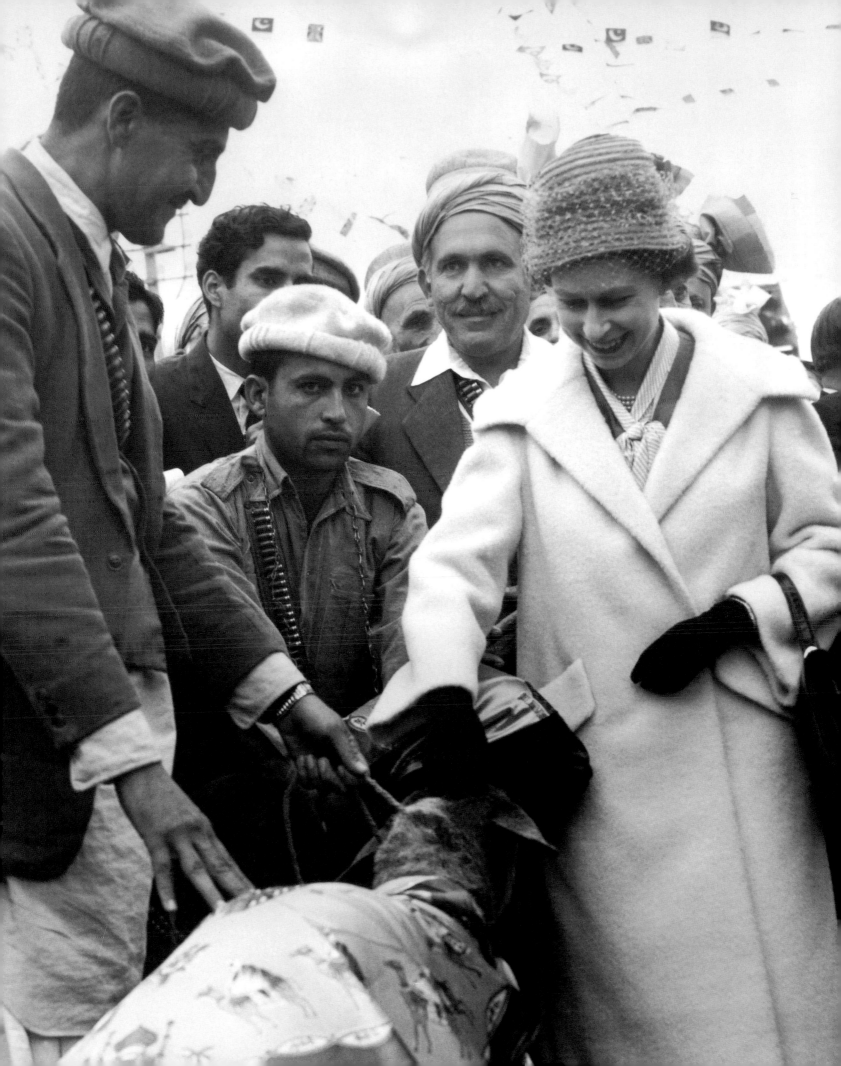

And what better way to be seen than on an elelphant? This was surely one of the most exotic journeys of her tour.

Looking magnificent in black lace and diamonds, the Queen went to the Vatican for a meeting with Pope John XXIII during a state visit to Italy in 1961.

Prince Philip – always drawn by a pretty face
– chats with Jackie Kennedy, while the
Queen and US President John Kennedy
prepare for photos at Buckingham Palace
in June 1961. Jackie came in for some
stick the next day when the British
press accused her of wearing a dress
that upstaged the Queen's Hartnell gown.

The final day of the Royal Ascot meeting,
June 1961, and Elizabeth, hard hat as usual
conspicuous by its absence, enjoys a gallop
on the course before the day's racing begins.

Elizabeth enjoys dancing. Here, she is partnered by Ghana's
President Kwame Nkrumah, doing "the shuffle" at a farewell ball at
the end of her tour of the West African state in November 1961.

Sierra Leone, December 1961. Wearing full evening dress, including long gloves and a tiara, Elizabeth has a word with her husband as they watch a display by traditional Susu dancers.

THE SECOND DECADE

1962–1971

THE SWINGING SIXTIES saw a bevy of royal babies: four years after Andrew's birth, the Queen had a fourth child, Edward, born on March 10, 1964, ten days after Princess Alexandra had her son James, and a couple of months before both the Duchess of Kent and Princess Margaret had babies. The Queen's eldest two, meanwhile, had become the first royal children to be sent to school rather than be educated at home. Unhappily for Charles, he was enrolled at his father's old school Gordonstoun, where he was utterly miserable, while Anne enjoyed happier times at a girls' boarding school, Benenden. As the Beatles strutted their stuff and flower power ruled, Charles did manage the odd moment of rebellion. In June 1963, aged fourteen, he was spotted in a cocktail bar in Stornaway sipping a cherry brandy. What his mother thought of this was not revealed, but as headmasterly canings threatened, newspapers had a field day: "Bend Over, Your Royal Highness!" was just one of the many headlines the next morning.

At the end of the first decade of Elizabeth's reign, undiluted glamour had come to visit in the shape of America's President Kennedy and his wife Jackie. In sad contrast, at the end of 1963, the Queen attended a memorial service in London for the assassinated President.

At Downing Street, Prime Ministers came and went: Harold Macmillan, who had succeeded Anthony Eden after the Suez Crisis, resigned in

1963 for health reasons. In a highly unusual meeting, the Queen went to see him in hospital where she listened to his advice about his successor. The popular choice of Rab Butler was shunned in favour of the aristocrat Lord Home. The Conservatives lost a General Election the following year, bringing the Labour Party, led by Harold Wilson, to power for the first time in the Queen's reign. It was the start of a rather fond relationship between the monarch and her new Prime Minister. They were socially and politically worlds apart, but, curiously, found enjoyment in their work together.

In 1965, the Queen bade farewell to Sir Winston Churchill, another Prime Minister who had won her affection in the early years of her reign. He died in January at the great age of ninety and, as a mark of the respect in which she and the nation held the great war leader, the Queen authorized a full state funeral. She herself led the mourners at St Paul's Cathedral.

The following day she and Prince Philip flew to Ethiopia at the start of a tour that would also take them to Sudan.

Shortly after their return from Africa a private message was delivered to Buckingham Palace. It was from a friend of the Queen's estranged uncle, the Duke of Windsor. Now seventy-one, he was in London for an eye operation. His wife Wallis was with him. The note read that the Duke would be "cheered and invigorated" by a visit from members of his family. After taking soundings from her mother and various advisers, the Queen drove to the London Clinic to see her uncle and – for the first time in twenty-nine years – to meet her "aunt". It was a stiff and formal encounter that lasted little more than twenty minutes, but it broke the long silence.

There was fence-mending to be done further afield as well. The twentieth anniversary of the end of the Second World War was looming and, after much prevarication, it was decided that the Queen should pay a state visit to Germany, the first by a British monarch for fifty-six years. It was a delicate mission and a controversial one, which drew more media attention than any tour since her Coronation. The Queen and Duke were given a noisy and enthusiastic welcome throughout the ten-day trip. It ended in Hanover where university students held up banners, which read: "We want you to invade us. We love your Queen. We want her for us."

Six months later she felt rather less loved by the Government of Rhodesia (now Zimbabwe) when its Prime Minister, Ian Smith, shocked the world by declaring independence from Britain. In spite of a formal proclamation from the Queen that Mr Smith and his ministers would forthwith cease to hold office, coupled with a flurry of international sanctions, Rhodesia's illegal regime survived for eleven years.

A clear function of the Crown is to be a rallying point at times of national rejoicing or tragedy. In 1966, the Queen was present for both. She's not a natural soccer fan but, in July, she watched with pride as England won the World Cup at Wembley. Three months later she surveyed the horror of a collapsed slag heap in the mining village of Aberfan in south Wales. A hundred-and-forty-six people, mostly children attending the village school, were killed, buried under hundreds of thousands of tonnes of rubble. The Queen told the dozens of bereaved parents that, as a mother, she was trying to understand what they were going through: "I'm sorry," she said, "but I can give you nothing at present except sympathy."

The following year came another gesture from the Royal Family aimed at healing old wounds. The Duchess of Windsor was invited to accompany her husband to the unveiling of a plaque in memory of Queen Mary. It was the first time since the abdication that Wallis had been included in a family gathering. She exchanged a few words with the Queen and the Queen Mother – who later went to the races, leaving the Duke and Duchess to make their way back to Paris.

The slight thaw in family relationships was matched by a gradual change in the way the Palace conducted its media policy. The Queen's press secretary of the past two decades, Commander Richard Colville, who had more or less dedicated his life to keeping the press out, retired in 1968. He was replaced by William Heseltine, an Australian who embraced the revolutionary idea that the Palace should work with the media instead of against them. He began to engineer photo calls and to allow television cameras into state occasions like banquets. It was heady stuff, and it culminated in a film that showed royalty as it had never been seen before.

Royal Family took viewers inside the Palace walls to watch the family at work and play. They were filmed on royal tours, at official engagements, shopping in a village store and having a barbecue by a Scottish loch. Though they were painfully self-conscious about the cameras, the Queen and her family suddenly seemed a little more human. When the film was shown on television – twice in eight days – an estimated forty million people tuned in and it received rave reviews. It also left the media baying for more – the genie was out of the bottle.

A week later, on July 1, 1969, a royal spectacular tailor-made for television was staged at Caernarvon Castle in Wales. The time had come for the Queen to launch her son and heir into his role as Prince of Wales. It was only the second time in three centuries that such an Investiture ceremony had been held and it was re-structured for the television age by Charles's uncle, Lord Snowdon, who was Constable of the

Castle. It turned out to be a strange mix of modern and medieval pageantry, and it was watched by millions around the world.

Problems with the royal finances also became public knowledge in these years. *The Times* newspaper reported that the Queen was overspending her allowance from the Civil List. Prince Philip went further; on American television he said the Royal Family would soon go into the red. "We may have to move to smaller premises, who knows?" he said, adding that he'd already been forced to sell a small yacht and might even have to give up polo. If he was looking for public sympathy, arguments like that were certainly not the most persuasive way of getting it. Nevertheless, in 1971, the Government doubled the Queen's Civil List to £980,000 a year, with an extra £255,000 to cover the expenses of other members of her family. But the pay rise wasn't approved without stinging criticism from a number of MPs and blunt debate in the papers about whether the monarchy was value for money.

Two decades into her reign, the Queen was learning that her efforts to make the monarchy more accessible had not put it beyond reproach.

Never more relaxed than at horsey events
or the racecourse, the Queen watches the
1962 Badminton Horse Trials from the
vantage point of a pile of hay bales. As usual,
several members of her family are with her.

A wonderful portrait of the Queen at work: Elizabeth
chats with Chelsea Pensioners at the Royal Hospital in
1962. The occasion was the annual Oak Apple Day parade
which marks the anniversary of the restoration of
Charles II, who founded the hospital in 1682.

What do you say to a sheep shearer? The Queen
and Duke find the appropriate words to
congratulate the winners of a shearing contest in
Wellington during a visit to New Zealand in 1963.

It's far cry from cruises on *Britannia*; the Queen drops in on a Butlin's holiday camp at Pwllheli in Wales in August 1963. At her side, the man who made it all happen, Billy Butlin.

The Queen with her youngest – and favourite – child, Edward Anthony Richard Louis on her knee, on the day of his christening in 1964. Prince Andrew rests his head on the arm of the sofa. Edward's birth was welcomed by the Archbishop of Canterbury, Dr Ramsay, with words he might have come to rue, had he still been Archbishop in the 1990s: "It means so much that at a time when not all homes are so lucky, there is around the throne a Christian family united, happy and setting to all an example of what the words 'home and family' most truly mean."

Malta re-visited in 1964. Elizabeth and Philip
recapture the carefree mood of their days
on the island before she became Queen.

Taking the children to work. The Queen and Prince Philip on the balcony of Buckingham Palace after the Trooping the Colour ceremony in June 1964. Four-year-old Prince Andrew waves to the crowds, while Edward, aged three months, only has eyes for his mum.

October, 1964. Home at last! After a controversial tour of Canada, during which the Queen faced noisy demonstrations by Quebec separatists, she's welcomed back to Britain by crowds intent on getting as close as they possibly can.

The Queen leaves the London Clinic in March 1965 after visiting her uncle, the Duke of Windsor, who was there for an eye operation. The visit broke a silence of twenty-nine years when she also met Wallis, Duchess of Windsor, the woman for whom her uncle had given up the throne in 1936.

The Queen in relaxed mood at home with her children in April 1965. The photograph was taken to mark her thirty-ninth birthday.

Previous pages: The Queen and Prince Philip among the mourners at the State Funeral of her first Prime Minister, Sir Winston Churchill, in January 1965. As a young monarch, she had respected his experience and knowledge, while he had thought her "quite splendid".

Ever ready with her camera, the Queen shoots a roll of film at the Badminton Horse Trials in 1965. Princess Anne, who would later become a very successful three-day event competitor, takes an equally keen interest. The Duke of Beaufort, owner of the Badminton estate and founder of the Horse Trials, sits next to the Queen.

The Queen and Duke of Edinburgh survey the Berlin Wall during their historic state visit to West Germany in May 1965. High in their watchtower in the East, the guards survey the Royal cavalcade through binoculars.

A countrywoman through and through, the Queen relaxes at Retriever Trials on Deeside in October 1965. One of her black labradors competed in the Novice Stakes that day.

A visit to the Isle of Wight in July 1965. The Queen stops for a chat with the island's oldest resident, one-hundred-and-five-year-old Frederick Yelf.

In the mid-1960s a film premiere became a very grand event when the Queen attended. Here she wears some of her most spectacular jewellery and the ribbon and badge of the Order of the Garter as well as family orders to attend the premiere of *Born Free*, the film of Joy Adamson's famous book about her work with lions in Africa.

She's no soccer fan, but this was a day for national
rejoicing as the Queen presents England captain
Bobby Moore with the Jules Rimet Trophy
after their dramatic defeat of Germany in
the final of the 1966 World Cup at Wembley.

The horror of Aberfan. The Queen in the midst of the bereaved Welsh mining community after a slag heap collapsed in October 1966, killing one-hundred-and-forty-six people, most of them children at school.

Showing off her muscles! The Queen cuts a giant cake to mark the centenary of Canada's confederation, July 1967.

For a few hours, Wallis Simpson is allowed into the royal fold. Her husband the Duke of Windsor, the exiled former King, bows to his niece and sovereign. The occasion is the unveiling of a plaque in June 1967 to commemorate the centenary of the birth of the Duke's mother, Queen Mary.

It was, they said, the picture that needed no headline. Using Sir Francis Drake's sword, the Queen knights Francis Chichester in July 1967 after his solo voyage around the world in *Gypsy Moth IV*. The outdoor ceremony at Greenwich was a television gimmick designed to show that the Palace was moving with the times.

September 1967 in Scotland, and the Queen is dwarfed by the towering bows of the brand new liner, the *QE II*. The Queen stands on the launching platform as the ship glides slowly down the slipway on Clydebank.

On the eve of her forty-second birthday, the Queen takes a break from worries about world events as she watches the 1968 Badminton Horse Trials with her husband. This was the year in which Martin Luther King was murdered and Senator Robert Kennedy was shot dead after an election rally. And it was a year in which the war in Vietnam dominated the world's news.

Elizabeth offers some tips on go-karting
to Charles and Edward at the wheel
of their new toy in April, 1969.

Overleaf: The Investiture of the Prince
of Wales at Caernarvon Castle in July 1969.
In a ceremony tailored for television, the Queen
formally installed Charles as Prince of Wales.
Both were struggling not to laugh because, in the
rehearsal, the crown had been too big and had
"extinguished the Prince like a candle-snuffer!"

This scene from the hugely successful 1969 television film, *Royal Family*, shows the older members of the Elizabeth's immediate family having a meal together. It was a public relations exercise they came to regret.

In this scene from *Royal Family*, the Queen is clearly at ease with her Prime Minister, Harold Wilson.

Trying to appear relaxed though in fact they all
look slightly uncomfortable with their situation,
the Queen, Prince Philip and their children
appear in another scene from *Royal Family*.

Charles and Anne show they're quite
willing to get their hands dirty as the family
help clear a wood on the Royal estates.

Girl guides together! The Queen and Princess Margaret – both former guides – join chief guide, Lady Olave Baden-Powell, at the Diamond Jubilee celebrations of the Girl Guides Association.

A word in your ear, young man! The Queen with her two youngest sons, Andrew, 11, and Edward, 7, in April 1971. Both boys seem to be less enthusiastic than their mother about the prospect of watching another horse show.

Given the choice the Queen would spend all day with her horses. Here at Windsor in 1971, about to ride out with the Duke of Edinburgh.

THE THIRD DECADE

1972–1981

AFTER TWENTY YEARS on the throne, the Queen had visited more than sixty countries and acquired a wide experience of world affairs. At home she had navigated a steady course through constitutional crises, and had listened to and counselled six Prime Ministers. Her family life seemed calm. Her eldest son came through his difficult school years, enjoyed life as a Cambridge undergraduate and was now serving in the Navy. Her daughter won acclaim as a horsewoman and, in 1971, had been voted BBC Sports Personality of the Year. The Queen's two youngest children were growing up with a mother who was more at ease with herself and who found more time for them than she had for their elder siblings. Her sister was safely married and her husband had settled into his role.

In 1972 Elizabeth and Philip celebrated their Silver Wedding Anniversary. On November 20, at a lunch at Guildhall to mark the occasion, the Queen allowed her dry humour to surface, taking a dig at those who had laughed over the years at her standard way of starting speeches, especially when Philip was with her. "I think everybody really will concede that on this of all days I should begin my speech with the words 'My husband and I'," she said. It brought the house down.

Elizabeth reflected, too, on family life. She told the assembled guests,

When the bishop was asked what he thought about sin he replied with simple conviction that he was against it. If I am asked today what I think about family life after twenty five years of marriage, I can answer with equal simplicity and conviction. I am for it.

Six months earlier the family had joined together to mourn the death of the Duke of Windsor, the former Edward VIII. His body was brought from Paris to lie in state at St George's Chapel, where sixty thousand people filed past. The Duchess was invited to stay at Buckingham Palace. After the years of alienation it was never going to be anything other than awkward: Wallis seemed disorientated and the Queen formal. After the funeral, the Duchess returned speedily to Paris, where she was quoted as complaining that none of the Royal Family had offered her any real sympathy.

In the summer of 1972 there was a more tragic death in the family. The Queen's cousin, Prince William of Gloucester, was killed in a flying accident. But there was happiness to come a year later when Princess Anne married a fellow horse trials competitor, Captain Mark Phillips.

After the wedding, the Queen flew to the South Seas for an extensive tour, leaving behind a country beset by industrial troubles. The Prime Minister was Edward Heath, who had taken the United Kingdom into the EEC in January 1973 and was now embroiled in a struggle with the trade unions that led, in February 1974, to his calling a snap general election, the theme of which was "Who rules Britain, government or unions?"

The Queen returned to Britain in time for the election result. An overall winner did not emerge, and the Queen found herself involved in a constitutional crisis. Mr Heath spent four days trying to persuade the Liberals to strike up a coalition with his Conservative Party; they refused and he resigned. The Queen sent for Harold Wilson again.

With the process of democracy duly back on track, she resumed her tour. She was in Indonesia when a call came through with alarming news. A gunman had tried to kidnap Princess Anne in the Mall. She'd been on her way back to Buckingham Palace with her husband when a Ford Escort cut in front of their car and a man jumped out firing a volley of shots. The Princess's protection officer, her driver and a passing journalist who went to

help were all injured; a policeman who ran across from St James's Palace was shot in the liver. Eventually the gunman, Ian Ball, was overpowered; his plan to demand a ransom for the Princess had been thwarted – but only just. He was committed to a psychiatric hospital indefinitely.

In 1975 a constitutional crisis in Australia re-opened the debate about the role of the monarchy there. It was a debate that had been rumbling in many Commonwealth countries since the UK had first tried to join the EEC. The Queen's representative in Australia, the Governor-General, Sir John Kerr, sacked the Prime Minister, Gough Whitlam, after he failed to get his Government's Budget through Parliament. It was a dramatic move – and fuelled calls for Australia to become a republic.

By 1976, the Queen's problems were more personal than constitutional. There were serious troubles in her family. In January 1976 Princess

Margaret flew to her holiday home in Mustique with her lover, Roddy Llewellyn. They'd been before and the media hadn't noticed – even though there had been rumours for some time about problems in the Princess's marriage. This time, a journalist was waiting and pictures of the happy couple sitting together in their swimming costumes were flashed around the world. On March 16, Buckingham Palace announced Princess Margaret and Lord Snowdon's separation. Although, in words that were to become all too familiar, the Palace insisted that there were no plans for divorce, the marriage was legally ended two years later. Unable to marry a divorced man twenty years earlier, the Princess had now brought divorce into the very heart of the royal family.

There was cause for national celebration in 1977, however. This year saw the Silver Jubilee of the Queen's reign. Initial doubts about whether the country was in a mood to party quickly faded as the Queen criss-crossed her realm on a Jubilee tour. To her own constant amazement, big crowds turned out and their enthusiasm proved contagious. Jubilee Day itself was a national holiday and a million people converged on Buckingham Palace to watch the Queen and Duke make their way to St Paul's Cathedral in the Gold State Coach. In a speech at Guildhall, she recalled the pledge she had made when she was twenty-one to dedicate her life to the service of her people. "Although that vow was made in my salad days when I was green in judgement, I do not regret one word of it."

Thousands of street parties were held around the country and messages of congratulation came in from all over the world at the rate of 1,000 an hour. As one newspaper put it, there was a feeling that "The Queen rules, UK."

The icing on the cake for the Queen in her Jubilee Year was that she became a grandmother. Princess Anne's son, Peter, came into the world on November 15 to headlines proclaiming "The Queen's Pride and Joy". And so he has proved.

This was also the decade that gave Britain its first woman Prime Minister. Margaret Thatcher was summoned to the Palace on May 4, 1979 after the Conservatives had comprehensively beaten James Callaghan's struggling Labour Party.

Three months later, tragedy struck the Royal Family when Lord Mountbatten, known to them all as Uncle Dickie, was assassinated by the IRA at Mullaghmore in the Republic of Ireland. A bomb hidden in his boat was detonated, killing Mountbatten, one of his grandsons and an Irish boy who'd been crewing. Mountbatten's daughter, Patricia, and her husband, Lord Brabourne were badly injured. Lord Brabourne's mother died a few hours later. It was a deadly blow to the family; Mountbatten had been a father figure to Prince Philip and a mentor to Prince Charles – who wrote that life would never be the same again.

Two women, one very old and one very young, dominated the final years of the Queen's third decade. In 1980 the Queen Mother celebrated her eightieth birthday with a special service at St Paul's. At the same time, speculation grew that Prince Charles had finally got marriage on his mind. Suddenly all eyes, and cameras, were fixed on nineteen-year-old Lady Diana Spencer. "Charlie's Girl!" the papers trumpeted as they captured the rather shy young woman at the kindergarten where she was working. Before long they got confirmation.

"My Di!" was the simple headline above the engagement photo of the Prince and his fiancée in February 1981. But were they in love? That was a question the troubled Prince found hard to answer in a television interview to mark the occasion. "Of course!" replied Lady Diana, looking slightly affronted. "Whatever 'in love' means," added her husband-to-be, looking uneasy.

Regardless of any doubts harboured by bride or groom, the wedding itself was, in the words of the Archbishop of Canterbury, the stuff of which fairytales are made. Six hundred thousand people lined the route and a billion watched on television; the nation took its new Princess to its heart. On that late July day, there was no inkling that this was in fact the start of the most turbulent period of the Queen's reign.

An awkward family group at the funeral
of the Duke of Windsor in June 1972.
Elizabeth, Prince Philip and the Queen
Mother endeavour to behave correctly
towards a disorientated Duchess of Windsor.

One of a series of official photographs taken to mark the Queen and Prince Philip's Silver Wedding anniversary in 1972, this picture brings the couple and all four of their children together in the garden at Balmoral Castle in Scotland. They had been through some rocky times, but now their life seemed settled and their children were not yet giving them cause for concern.

Another picture of royal togetherness. Here, the Queen watches Philip practise his angling skills.

It's April 1973, and Princess Anne has graduated from spectator to competitor at the annual Badminton Horse Trials. It's looking tense as the family watch her competing in one of the phases of the gruelling event. The Queen, her mother and Prince Edward (at the back) are joined by Lord Snowdon and his two children, David and Sarah, to cheer Anne on.

With her camera ready for action, the Queen lets herself enjoy a big laugh at the Windsor Horse Show, in May 1973. It's always been one of the most informal of royal occasions: the Queen and her family like to mingle with as little fuss as possible.

Another photograph from the Windsor Horse
Show in 1973. Surrounded, as always, by her corgis,
the Queen takes a back seat away from the crowds.

The first of the Queen's brood to fly the nest:
newlyweds Princess Anne and Captain Mark Phillips
on the Buckingham Palace balcony after their wedding at
Westminster Abbey, November 14, 1973. The ceremony was
watched by 500 million television viewers around the world.

Girls' night out: the
Queen and her daughter
greet one another at the
premiere of the film
*Murder on the Orient
Express* in 1974.

Facing middle age. With her husband and youngest son, the Queen celebrates her fiftieth birthday at Windsor Castle in 1976.

The balcony scene at Buckingham Palace that has come to epitomise great national occasions and royal celebrations: this one for the Queen's Silver Jubilee in June, 1977. From the left: Prince Charles, Prince Edward, Prince Andrew, Earl Mountbatten, The Queen and Duke, Captain Mark Phillips and Princess Anne

Not since the celebrations that marked the
end of the Second World War had Britain
seen so many street parties as it did in the
summer of 1977. After a rather slow start, the
nation entered wholeheartedly into celebrating
the Silver Jubilee of the Queen's accession.
This get-together was at Woodbridge in Essex.

At the Silver Jubilee service of thanksgiving at St Paul's Cathedral the Queen had appeared tense at times. One newspaper commented that she'd looked "cheesed off". Once outside with the crowds, however, she seemed at last to be truly enjoying the celebrations.

What better year for a British champion at Wimbledon? Virginia Wade provided the icing on the Silver Jubilee cake with an historic win in the Ladies' Singles Final. The Queen, a very infrequent visitor to the world-famous tennis championships, was there to present the trophy.

The Queen became a grandmother in her Silver Jubilee year, when Princess Anne gave birth to a son, Peter, on November 15, 1977. Here, she admires her grandson, in his mother's arms, after his christening at Buckingham Palace in December.

Elizabeth and Prince Philip walk
with Kuwait's Defence Minister, Salem
Sabah, beneath the dramatic Kuwait Towers
during a visit in 1979 to the oil-rich Arab state.

Fresh air, the family and – of course – the dogs!
The Queen relaxes with her brood at Balmoral
in 1979. Her Scottish home provides refuge
from public life for many weeks every year.

April, 1980, and its Badminton Horse Trials time again. The Queen has never been simply an idle spectator at this, the biggest event of the British three-day eventing year. She knows the background and abilities of every horse in the event, and of most of the competitors, too. Her knowledge of horses is admired by everyone in the business.

Grief is etched on the faces of the Royal Family at the funeral service of Earl Mountbatten of Burma, Westminster Abbey, September 5, 1979. From the left: Princess Anne, the Queen Mother, Captain Mark Phillips, the Queen, Prince Charles, Princess Margaret, Prince Andrew, wearing the uniform of a Royal Navy midshipman for the first time in public, Prince Philip and Prince Edward.

The Queen Mother in party mood as her daughter and the rest of the Royal Family join her at Clarence House to celebrate her eightieth birthday, August 4, 1980.

The Queen comes close to a fit of the giggles as she struggles to keep her feathers on after the annual service of the Order of the Garter in St George's Chapel, Windsor in 1980. Prince Charles has already surrendered to the gales and taken off his hat while the Queen Mother gallantly hangs on to hers. Also with the royal party: the Queen of Denmark and the Grand Duke of Luxembourg.

Backstage at Buckingham Palace on her wedding day, July 29, 1981. Diana takes time to reassure her young bridesmaids.

Drama at the Trooping the Colour ceremony in June 1981: the Queen is pictured moments after a man in the crowd fired six shots from a starting pistol. Her riding expertise enabled her to control her frightened horse, Burmese, without difficulty. The papers called it "the awful moment when it seemed that the Queen had been shot".

On the balcony at Buckingham Palace after their wedding, Prince Charles kisses the hand of his young bride. When they exchanged a real kiss a few seconds later, the thousands gathered in the Mall outside the palace roared their approval.

THE FOURTH DECADE

1982–1991

ELIZABETH HAD BEEN QUEEN for thirty years and was a well-respected, if sometimes remote, figurehead. In 1982, however, she shared an experience that brought her much closer to the nation. Like so many other mothers, she had to watch as her son went to war. Prince Andrew, now twenty-two, was a helicopter pilot on HMS *Invincible* when the Falklands conflict began. On April 2, Argentine troops invaded the islands by air and sea. Two days later a British task force led by *Invincible* and other warships sailed from Portsmouth for the South Atlantic. As Queen, she felt responsible for all the troops who had been dispatched to defend crown and country. As a mother she worried about her son, who faced real danger in the ensuing months. By September though, Andrew was home – red rose in his mouth and fist punching the air – to a hero's welcome.

Much had happened in his absence. In June there had been a newcomer to the Royal Family: Charles and Diana now had a son and heir. William was born on June 21, not at Buckingham Palace but in a London hospital. Prince Charles emerged from the hospital elated but tired, and announced that the baby had the "good fortune" not to look like him. It had not been the easiest of pregnancies. The Princess, had come into the family at a young age, full of raw emotion, and was finding royal life not at all as she had expected. In a dramatic plea for attention, she'd thrown herself down the stairs at Sandringham during the early stage of her pregnancy. She told me later that it had not been a serious attempt to hurt herself or the baby; she'd meant it as a cry for help, but it had gone unheeded. It's certainly true that her husband did not know how to handle this volatile girl, already so damaged by her childhood. Diana could not suppress her suspicions that Charles was still in love with Camilla Parker Bowles. There were hopes that the new baby would settle things down.

The Queen herself had been quite unsettled by an astonishing breach of security at Buckingham Palace. One morning in early July she woke up to find an intruder in her bedroom. Michael Fagan, a thirty-one-year-old unemployed labourer, had scaled the Palace walls, climbed in through a window and wandered around for almost half an hour before coming across the Queen's bedroom. There was no-one on guard duty; the overnight shift had just ended. Fagan went in; the Queen was still asleep. When she opened her eyes to see this total stranger in her room she shouted at him to "get out at once". But he didn't; instead he sat on her bed, started talking about his family and asked for a cigarette. Incredibly, the alarm bell which the Queen immediately sounded went unheeded; so did two emergency phone calls to her security officers.

Finally, a chambermaid stumbled upon this most bizarre scene and blurted out "Oh, bloody 'ell Ma'am, what's 'e doing 'ere?" – a scene the Queen would later mimic with some amusement. Fagan was eventually grabbed by a footman and security at Buckingham Palace was given a thorough overhaul. It was certainly quite a story for the royal correspondents of the day!

They were occupied, too, with the growing signs of strain in the Wales's marriage. At a polo match in the summer of 1983, Prince Charles made headlines by shooting from the hip at a group of photographers "Get these bloody people out of the way," he shouted. "Bloody peeping toms. Why can't you leave my wife alone for one bloody second? Leave her alone for God's sake."

The Queen, though, has rarely interfered in the marriages of her children. The Royal Family is almost fanatically buttoned up about its emotions and Prince Charles was now viewed as master of his own household – and of any problems that came with it. The Queen was also busy with her own commitments at home and abroad. During the course of the 1980s she travelled extensively: to Australia (four times) and to the South Sea islands, to the Caribbean and the States, to Africa and India, to Portugal and China, to Malaysia and Singapore, to mention but a few. This was still the era of extended royal tours; some lasted five or six weeks – far longer than today – and the pace was often punishing. So, occasionally, was the press coverage the Queen and Duke received.

During their tour of Canada in 1984 the Queen was lambasted by the Canadian papers for being "dowdy and boring". They said her make-up was too heavy, her hats were awful and her legs had visible veins. It was all too much for the Daily Mirror which sprang to her defence with a blunt front page: "DON'T BE SO BLOODY RUDE!"

There was, however, no such defence of the Duke when he remarked to some British students in China that they would get "slitty eyes" if they stayed too long. It went down as one of his biggest clangers and even caused the Foreign Secretary, Sir Geoffrey Howe, to issue an apology. Increasingly, this was becoming the decade when the media cast aside their rose-tinted spectacles and put the role, value and demeanour of the Royal Family under critical scrutiny.

Shortly before their Canadian visit, the Queen and Duke had became grandparents again, Diana having given birth to her second son, Prince Henry – always called Harry – in September 1984. No doubt they both hoped that the new baby signalled more tranquil times ahead; sadly the opposite was true. By now the Wales's marriage was virtually over in all but name.

In 1986, as the Queen celebrated her sixtieth birthday, another addition to the family romped on to the scene in the shape of a flame-haired bundle of fun named Sarah Ferguson. She'd won the heart of the Queen's second son, Andrew, and on July 23 they were married at Westminster Abbey, emerging as the Duke and Duchess of York. Although Sarah Ferguson was not quite the usual cut of royal bride – like most modern women in their late twenties, she'd had previous lovers – she enjoyed a honeymoon period with the public and media who viewed her as a breath of fresh air. It was not to last – and neither was the marriage.

It was Prince Edward, however, who was to cause the next storm. After graduating from Cambridge he'd joined the Royal Marines, but he wasn't happy. Courageously, according to some – wimpishly, according to others – he suddenly announced he was quitting this rough, tough world of no-quitters. He wanted to go into the theatre. To prove he had what it takes, he decided to stage a charity TV spectacular, *It's a Royal Knock-Out*. He persuaded not only the Duke and Duchess of York to take part but, rather surprisingly, his sister as well – recently elevated to the status of Princess Royal and

normally so careful to avoid any television stunts. The Queen thought it was a bad idea but, reluctant as ever to upset her children, she allowed Edward to go ahead. It was shown in 1987 and was an unmitigated disaster. The Royal Family had become a laughing stock, struggling to hold their own as rather wooden television celebrities. When the media refused to praise Edward's efforts, the petulant Prince stormed out of a press conference, reinforcing the impression that he was arrogant, immature and spoiled.

If further evidence were needed that the Royal Family was not so very different from the rest of us, it was provided in 1989 by the Princess Royal. Her marriage was over, and the world learned that she and Mark Phillips were separating. What was more, there seemed to be someone else involved. Only a few months earlier, love letters to the Princess written by the Queen's equerry, Commander Tim Laurence, had been stolen and sent to a tabloid newspaper. Now, it was clear, the princess reciprocated his love.

Elizabeth must have viewed the end of the 1980s and the start of a new decade with mixed feelings. She'd been given a pay rise and the Civil List had been set for the next ten years, but despite her own unfailing dedication to her job, the Royal Family was increasingly lampooned as a soap opera. Her eldest son's marriage was in dire trouble, her daughter was separated and her youngest son was publicly mocked. She had two new grand-daughters, Beatrice and Eugenie, but there were obvious cracks in the Yorks' marriage too. Perhaps it was all summed up at the annual Royal Windsor Horse Show in 1991 when, almost on her own front doorstep, the Queen was refused entry to the private grandstand. "Sorry, love, you can't come in without a sticker," she was told by an officious security guard.

Explaining himself later to his bosses and waiting reporters, the embarrassed guard said; "I thought she was some old dear who'd got lost."

Before long, it would seem that the entire Royal Family had, indeed, lost its way.

Home from the Falklands! Prince Andrew enjoys the welcome home for HMS *Invincible* after the war in the South Atlantic. The rose was said to be a sign of his love for his girlfriend of the time, Koo Stark.

Royal transport with a difference: the Queen is carried in a ceremonial canoe on the shoulders of the islanders of Tuvalu during a tour of the South Pacific in 1982.

The Queen signs the repatriated Canadian Constitution as Canadian Prime Minister Pierre Trudeau looks on.

A rare public display of affection: Elizabeth and Philip say farewell as their official duties take them separate ways.

Prince William was christened at Buckingham
Palace in August 1982. Here, everyone acts their
part beautifully for the camera as "shy Di" sits centre
stage after the ceremony. But already the family was
beginning to wonder about how this volatile and
emotional girl would shape up as a future Queen.

Elizabeth and Prince Philip visited US President Ronald Reagan's home state of California in March 1983. At a dinner in San Francisco President Reagan finds something about the Queen vastly amusing; presumably it was not her extravagant dress – which was the talk of the banquet. Made of champagne silk taffeta, it had two huge shoulder bows and, with its feathered sleeves, was a contrast to her usual style.

Eyes up! On the balcony of Buckingham Palace after the Trooping the Colour, the Royal party turn their gaze skywards for a fly past by 61 Squadron of the Royal Airforce.

At Woolwich on the River Thames, May 8, 1984, the Queen opens the "eighth wonder of the world", the Thames Barrier, which was designed to protect London from floods.

Bayeux, France, June 6, 1984: forty years on, the Queen chats with veterans of the D-Day landings in Normandy. She also met some of the widows who were flown over for the ceremony honouring the war dead.

Wifely pride as Elizabeth applauds her husband's
success in the carriage-driving competition
at the Windsor Horse Show in May 1985.

And maternal pride too. Their relationship
may not be close, but it is always polite.
Here, in July 1985, in his polo-playing heyday,
Prince Charles kisses his mother's hand after
accepting the trophy for his winning team.

Outside Buckingham Palace on April 21, 1986:
it is her sixtieth birthday and Elizabeth has plenty
to smile about as she accepts flowers from some
of the six thousand schoolchildren who brought
daffodils and songs to wish her a happy anniversary.

July 1986: the start of another Royal marriage that seemed so full of promise. Sarah Ferguson, the new Duchess of York, takes her place on the Palace balcony for the first time. The crowds below loved her.

Inspecting an unusual guard of honour, the terracotta warriors in the city of X'ian, during the state visit to China in 1986. It was there that Prince Philip is said to have made his notorious "slitty eyes" comment – earning himself the label the "Great Wally of China".

Command performance: the Queen with
Cher and Steven Spielberg at the royal premiere
of *Empire of the Sun* in London in 1988.

Epsom, June 1988: one's won! Even one of the richest women in the world enjoys a win at the races. The Queen shows her delight as 15–8 favourite Waajib hits the front in the 2.45 on Derby Day. Just missing being hit by the royal race card is Prince Michael of Kent.

In 1989, the year that Communism was brought down by a wave of people power, the Soviet leader Mikhail Gorbachev was the Queen's guest at Windsor. They agreed that she would visit Moscow – though no date was set.

The Queen at her most casual at the Windsor Horse Show in May, 1988. She holds her spectacles which, by this time in her life, she needed for reading but not for wearing all the time.

There's not much that will keep the Queen from the races – certainly not the small matter of chilly, wet weather. This is Derby Day, 1990 and both the Queen and Prince Philip top their macs with smart hats as they stride out at Epsom.

THE FIFTH DECADE

1992–2002

THE YEAR THAT MARKED the fortieth anniversary of the Queen's Accession was also her bleakest. One calamity after another struck the Royal Family and by the end of 1992 the Queen herself had named it her "*annus horribilis*".

It was the year that three royal marriages hit the rocks. In March the Duke and Duchess of York separated; in April the Princess Royal divorced Mark Phillips and – most shocking of all – the separation of the Prince and Princess of Wales was announced in December. Around these events came the explosive book, *Diana: Her True Story*, by Andrew Morton in which Diana poured out her heart; the excruciating pictures of a topless Fergie having her toes sucked by her "financial adviser"; leaked phone conversations, first between Diana and a male friend, then between Prince Charles and Camilla Parker-Bowles; and, the final blow, a devastating fire at Windsor Castle. When the Heritage Secretary rode to the rescue, declaring that the Government would pay the repair bill, public uproar ensued. It was an agonizing time for the Queen, as the edifice of home and family crumbled about her.

Four days after the fire at the Castle, I sat in Guildhall along with the great and the good of the City of London who were gathered to celebrate the Queen's four decades on the throne. As she rose to her feet, looking wan and fragile, I prepared to take notes. This, we had been warned, would be a speech that mattered. Her voice was cracked – from the effects of a cold as well as emotion – and she seemed small and vulnerable. "1992 is not a year on which I shall look back with undiluted pleasure," she said. "In the words of one of my more sympathetic correspondents, it has turned out to be an *annus horribilis*."

She wondered how future generations would judge the events of that "tumultuous" year and hoped that they might show more compassion and wisdom than contemporary commentators. She was, though, prepared to show a measure of humility:

> There can be no doubt, of course, that criticism is good for people and institutions that are part of public life. No institution – City, monarchy whatever – should expect to be free from the scrutiny of those who give it their loyalty and support, not to mention those who don't.

However, she'd clearly been stung by the avalanche of criticism and ridicule to which her family had been subjected. In a plea for a kinder press, she said there was no reason for scrutiny to be less effective if it were made with a touch of gentleness, good humour and understanding.

The sole bright spot in the Queen's year came at the very end, when her daughter Anne remarried in a quiet ceremony in Scotland. What a long way the royal family had come: with divorce and re-marriage now accepted. And what a leap the Princess's new husband Tim Laurence had made: from equerry to royal spouse.

This was the decade when the Palace locked horns with its critics in a battle to win over public opinion. First, the Queen began paying income tax; then the doors of Buckingham Palace were thrown open to summer visitors to help pay for the fire damage at Windsor. It was intended as a temporary measure, but the Palace tour has since become one of London's most popular attractions.

The Prince of Wales's team decided that they, too, would woo the public by allowing a camera team to follow Charles for a major documentary about his life and work. However, when the programme, *Charles: The Private Man, the Public Role*, was broadcast in 1994 it wasn't the Prince's work that people were interested in – it was his frank admission that he had committed adultery. The film, and the book that followed, overshadowed the Queen's historic visit to Russia and left the royal family looking more dysfunctional than ever.

An equally historic visit the following year went ahead in calmer waters and with huge success. The Queen instantly warmed to the ebullient President of post-apartheid South Africa, Nelson Mandela. She held a media reception on board the royal yacht, Britannia, and told us how enthralled she was to be back in Cape Town. It was, she said, so full of memories of her only other tour of South Africa, in 1947 with her parents.

However, another television programme was soon to rock the monarchy to its foundations. To the astonishment and horror of the Queen and her household, the Princess of Wales secretly gave a lengthy interview to the BBC's *Panorama*. In a dramatic performance she opened up her heart and took several carefully scripted swipes at her estranged husband. She said her marriage had always been crowded – a reference to Camilla Parker Bowles; she admitted her own adultery with an army officer Major James Hewitt; and, unforgivably in the eyes of the Palace, she questioned whether Prince Charles was cut out to be King. The Queen acted swiftly.

Breaking her own rule never to interfere in her children's private lives, she wrote to both Charles and Diana urging them to seek a divorce. A few months later, in the summer of 1996, their marriage was officially ended. The Duke and Duchess of York divorced in the same year.

If nothing else, domestic matters had at least been tidied up and the Queen could have been forgiven for thinking that her family was set on a steadier path. However, 1997 brought the most lethal blow of all. In the middle of the night at the end of August, a phone call ruptured the peace of Balmoral Castle. The Princess of Wales had been involved in a car crash in Paris. Her lover Dodi Fayed was dead and she was gravely injured. As the Queen and Prince Charles took in the shock of this, news came through that the Princess had died.

The week that followed was one of the most mutinous of the Queen's reign. A tidal wave of grief swept through the country, closely followed by rumblings of discontent over the absence of any broadcast or public show of emotion by the Queen. She judged that her place was at Balmoral protecting and comforting her grandsons, William and Harry, in their greatest hour of need. As the days went by, the rumblings became dangerously noisy. The newspapers spoke bluntly for the people: "WHERE IS OUR QUEEN?" they demanded.

At the eleventh hour, the Palace recognized the strength of public feeling. Protocol and tradition were jettisoned to allow the Union Flag to fly at half-mast over Buckingham Palace; the funeral route was lengthened to accommodate the crowds; and the Queen returned to London to walk among the mourners and address the nation. She did so, she said, "not only as your Queen but as a grandmother". She also made a crucial concession: that there were "lessons to be drawn from Diana's life and from the extraordinary and moving reaction to her death". It was a pivotal moment and she struck the right note. The very real fears that she might be booed at Diana's funeral faded.

There's no doubt that the Royal Family and the Palace courtiers were badly shaken by the way they misjudged the public mood. Years on, though, it's hard to gauge exactly what lessons have been learned from Diana's life and death. One change, it seems to me, is an added air of caution among the Queen's advisers: there is a nervousness about presuming the public will want to celebrate landmarks in the Royal Family's life. Less than three months after Diana's death, the Golden Wedding of the Queen and Duke was a particularly sensitive occasion. The crowds were comparatively small and the celebrations fairly low-key. Perhaps in an effort to appear less cold and remote, the Queen paid an unusually personal tribute to her husband. Philip, she said, had quite simply been "her strength and stay all these years".

The wedding of her youngest son, Prince Edward, was similarly low-key: at St George's Chapel in Windsor. There were hopes that his bride, Sophie Rhys-Jones, would be the new jewel in the crown of the monarchy. A modern career woman, she had been allowed to accustom herself to royal life gradually, virtually living with Prince Edward at Buckingham Palace. However, her determination to enhance her career in public relations, coupled with her husband's failing efforts to run a television production company, brought new trouble for the Queen. The lines became blurred: was this the new face of royalty or were they simply business executives trading on their status? It was a question that divided the family and wiped out the little public affection the newly created Earl and Countess of Wessex had accrued.

Genuine affection, though, brought some forty thousand people out onto the streets to celebrate the Queen Mother's one-hundredth birthday in the first summer of the new millennium. Thousands more re-grouped the following year to mark her one-hundred-and-first.

Like her mother, the Queen shows every sign of working on into late old age. As far as she's concerned, the job to which she dedicated herself when she was twenty-one is a commitment for life – but it has claimed a heavy toll. As a mother herself, for example, the Queen must sometimes wonder how well she has done. Why did three of her children find it impossible to make their marriages work? She is not a tactile woman and seems emotionally repressed. Did she give her children the love and affection they needed? Was she there when they wanted to be with her – or was she away on yet another foreign tour? As she heads into her late seventies, she cannot yet settle into the bosom of a happy and harmonious family. Her eldest son is in love with a woman who played a part in the break-up of his marriage. Although the Queen has finally extended a hand of friendship to Camilla Parker Bowles – inviting her to join family celebrations and occasionally to take a seat in the royal box – she remains deeply troubled by the implications of this relationship and the public response if Charles were to marry her. Prince Andrew, meanwhile, is still curiously attached to the woman he divorced – to the great consternation of the Duke of Edinburgh and the puzzlement of the Queen. Even the Princess Royal, widely admired for her hard work, has been rumoured to be unhappy in her second marriage, while the Earl and Countess of Wessex have struggled to overcome their reputation as avaricious opportunists, even though both finally gave up their jobs. It is not the family portrait the Queen would have wished for.

May 1992. Still sprightly at sixty-six – and in spite of the *annus horribilis*. The Queen skips off the royal barge on a visit to Malta and Gozo.

November 21, 1992. The day after fire destroyed a major part of Windsor Castle the Queen plods across the sodden lawns to see the damage to her home.

The grim reality of the fire damage: the Queen surveys the ruins of St George's Hall. Along with the rest of the castle the Hall has since been restored to its former glory in what has been called a triumph of British craftsmanship.

The Queen addresses the guests at the luncheon held at Guildhall on November 24, 1992 to celebrate the fortieth anniversary of her Accession. She seemed tiny and vulnerable as, in a hoarse voice, she reflected on the "*annus horribilis*" that 1992 had become for her.

Balmoral December 12, 1992. Happiness second time round? The wedding of the Princess Royal to Commander Tim Laurence: one of the few bright spots for the Queen in a dismal year.

In 1995, the Queen made a state visit to South Africa, her first since 1947. She was immediately captivated by the country's charismatic President, Nelson Mandela, all the more so because he had returned his country to the Commonwealth.

A hand of friendship in the Caribbean brings a smile to the Queen's face during a visit to Anguilla in February 1994.

With her daughter, the Queen lays a wreath at the gates of Dunblane Primary School in Scotland, where sixteen children and their teacher died after Thomas Hamilton went berserk with a gun in March 1996.

When the Queen made an historic state visit to Russia in October 1994, President Yeltsin escorted her through Moscow's Red Square. Security was so tight that very few ordinary Russians could get anywhere near her.

Proof of the outpouring of grief for a dead Princess. Back from Scotland on the eve of Diana's funeral, the Queen and the Duke of Edinburgh amid the ocean of tributes outside Buckingham Palace, September 5, 1997.

September 6, 1997. After a moving and dramatic funeral service for Diana, Princess of Wales, the Queen and Queen Mother watch in sorrow as her coffin is driven away from Westminster Abbey.

The Queen, Queen Mother and
Princess Margaret watch a flypast on
the fiftieth anniversary of VE day, May 1995.

Previous pages: Her face etched with grief,
and fighting back the tears, the Queen bids
farewell to the Royal Yacht as *Britannia*
is decommissioned. She was later criticized
for showing more emotion over the loss
of a yacht than she had at Diana's funeral.

The Queen, in socks, at the Golden Temple of Amritsar during her troubled tour of India and Pakistan in 1997.

Seeking guidance on the meaning of the dance: the Queen watches a cultural display beneath a giant banyan tree on the outskirts of Madras (now Chenai) during her Indian tour.

Despite the controversy that dogged the 1997 tour of India and Pakistan, the Queen managed a smile as she visited the spice market in the southern city of Kochin.

The Queen enjoys a chuckle at the service held in Westminster Abbey on November 20, 1997, to mark the Golden Anniversary of her wedding there in 1947. Her husband, sons and two of her grandsons get on with the serious business of singing.

They may be generations and lifestyles apart, but the Queen and singer Julia Thompson hit it off at a Buckingham Palace reception for the world of the performing arts in April 1998. Behind the Queen is the third Labour Prime Minister of her reign, Tony Blair, who had been elected less than a year before.

Dressed for the occasion! The Queen covers up for a visit to a Mosque during a three day tour to Brunei in September 1998.

A memorable moment in Malaysia, during the Queen's 1998 visit to South East Asia. A Royal autograph is quite a rarity, but thirteen-year-old Nicolas How struck lucky in Kuala Lumpur when the Queen agreed to sign his football. He belongs to the Malaysian Manchester United Football Club Supporters and the Queen seemed happy to oblige.

November 1998 in Buckingham Palace and Prince Charles thanks his mother for throwing a party to mark his fiftieth birthday. To much laughter he addressed her as "Mummy … coupled, of course with Your Majesty!" In fact relations between the two were particularly strained at this time because of her refusal to attend a party for the Prince organized by his partner, Camilla Parker Bowles.

The Queen at the wedding of her youngest
son, Prince Edward, to Sophie Rhys-Jones at
Windsor in June 1999. The invitations said
"no hats" – but the Queen couldn't resist a
few feathers. Prince Edward was given the title
Earl of Wessex and his wife became a Countess.

New Year's Eve, 2000, in the notorious Dome at Greenwich in London. A little unsure about how it's done? The Queen holds hands with the Prime Minister, Tony Blair, for "Auld Lang Syne" as midnight strikes to usher in the new millennium.

One hundred years old and still enjoying life to the full, the Queen Mother acknowledges the birthday greetings of the crowd, 40,000-strong, who joined in the celebrations outside Buckingham Palace on August 4, 2000. Princess Margaret, the Duke of Edinburgh and the Queen savour the moment.

The Princess Royal makes her parents laugh at a party to celebrate her fiftieth birthday at Windsor Castle in November 2000. Her husband, Tim Laurence, looks on. Many of the guests were from the large number of charities with which the Princess is connected.

What do you give a woman who has everything? The Pope comes up with an answer during the Queen's visit to the Vatican in October 2000: a copy of a thirteenth-century Bible.

The Duke of Edinburgh steps centre stage at a Windsor Castle party to mark his eightieth birthday. The Queen takes on that slightly shy, submissive look of a wife whose husband might say something outrageous at any moment.

Clarence House, August 4, 2001: a full family gathering for an extraordinary occasion: the Queen Mother's one-hundred-and-first birthday. Even though she had been in hospital for a blood transfusion a few days earlier, she insisted on going ahead with the celebrations.

Chastened by criticicism over her long reign that she has not always responded swiftly to tragic world events, the Queen broke her holiday at Balmoral to lead a memorial service for the thousands who died in the terrorist attack on the World Trade Centre in New York on September 11, 2001. It was held at St Paul's Cathedral, just three days after the events.

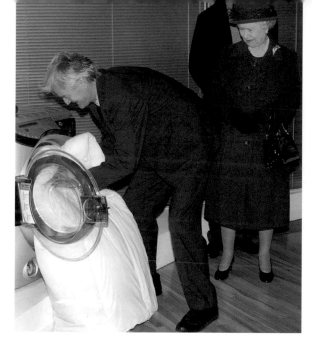

Unaccustomed as one is to washday drudgery ... the Queen looks suitably intrigued by James Dyson's demonstration of his new machine at his Wiltshire factory.

November 2001. Acknowledging the welcome from the crowds in Londonderry on her first visit there for almost half a century.

The closest the Queen has ever come to pulling a pint! On a day devoted to meeting people from the world of broadcasting, she almost became a soap Queen as she ventured behind the bar of the Queen Vic on the set of *Eastenders*. Showing her the ropes were Barbara Windsor (alias Peggy Mitchell) and Steve Mc Fadden (Phil Mitchell).

December 2001. The occasion was a celebration of Princess Alice's one hundredth birthday. It turned out, however, to be the last time Princess Margaret was seen in public. Two months later she suffered her third stroke and, after heart problems set in, she died in hospital aged seventy-one. Her funeral was held in St George's Chapel, Windsor fifty years to the day that her father had been buried in the same church.

February 6, 2002. The anniversary of her father's death and a day usually spent out of public view. But in her Golden Jubilee Year, the Queen marked her Accession day by visiting a Cancer Care Unit in King's Lynn, Norfolk. The choice was no coincidence: George VI had died fifty years earlier after a struggle against lung cancer.

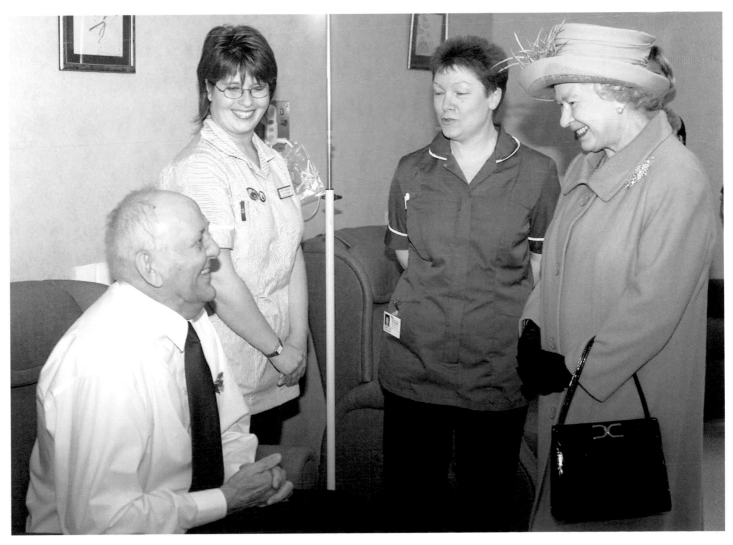

THE GOLDEN JUBILEE

2002

THE YEAR OF the Queen's Golden Jubilee turned out to be one of great joy and profound sadness. It also brought courtroom drama that once again rocked the monarchy to its roots.

At the beginning of 2002, no one seemed sure how the country would respond to this momentous anniversary in the Queen's reign. The Palace in particular proceeded with great caution, anxious not to presume that people would want to join in a national celebration. Their public stance was: party if you want to; if you don't, that's fine, too. Privately, of course, they acknowledged that the Jubilee would be a crucial test of twenty-first-century opinion.

The exact date of Elizabeth's accession has always been tinged with sadness. It was, of course, not only the day that she became Queen, but also the day on which her father died. Normally she spends the anniversary out of the public eye but, on February 6 of her Jubilee Year, she chose to open a new cancer unit in Norfolk. It was cold and the crowds were small; the media was quick to ask whether the Jubilee was going to be a flop. Apathy, some predicted, would be the dominant emotion.

Three days later, on February 9, it was announced that Princess Margaret had died. She was seventy-one. Even though she had suffered three strokes and had been ill for a long time, Margaret's death came as a shock to her family. It seemed so wrong: a mother losing her daughter, an elder sister mourning her sibling.

For the Queen Mother, now one-hundred-and-one, there was a further dilemma. Since Christmas she had been stranded at Sandringham – first by a chest infection and then by increasing frailty. How could she make the journey to Windsor for the Princess's funeral? Until the very last moment, it seemed that she would have to miss it. In the end, however, her steely determination saw her through. She flew to Windsor by helicopter and, in a wheelchair, was able to attend the funeral service at St George's Chapel in the castle precincts. It was one of the hardest duties a mother could be asked to perform and it took its toll.

Princess Margaret – who had sometimes behaved as the grandest of the royals – had requested a simple, private funeral, but around three thousand people lined the streets of Windsor to watch her coffin pass by. Breaking with royal tradition, she had also asked to be cremated so that her ashes could be placed in the tiny King George VI Chapel alongside her father – and, eventually, her mother. By an extraordinary quirk of fate, her funeral, on February 15, was held exactly fifty years to the day that her father was laid to rest. No wonder, then, that the Queen was seen to wipe away a tear.

It was a grim start to her Jubilee Year but, never a woman to put private grief before public duty, just three days after the funeral the Queen set off on an official visit to Jamaica, New

Zealand and Australia. It was not an easy time for her to be away from home, knowing that her mother was growing weaker by the day.

Four weeks after the Queen's return from her travels, she was warned by the doctors that they feared the Queen Mother would not survive the day. She hurried to her mother's bedside at Royal Lodge in Windsor Great Park and found her drifting in and out of consciousness. Close members of the family gathered round her bedside. At 3.15 on that Saturday afternoon, March 30, in the year of her daughter's Golden Jubilee, the Queen Mother's long life finally ebbed away.

It was, of course, inevitable – she was almost one-hundred-and-two – and yet it seemed strangely impossible. For most people, the Queen Mother had always been around, if only on the distant horizon of their lives. Suddenly she was gone, and there was genuine shock

As word of her death spread, people began to gather outside Buckingham Palace. The news had been announced in the traditional way on a billboard fixed to the railings. It said:

The Queen, with the greatest sadness, has asked for the following announcement to be made immediately. Her beloved mother, Queen Elizabeth, died peacefully this afternoon at Royal Lodge, Windsor.

In the ten days that followed, the country surprised itself, the pundits and even the Palace with a show of affection and sorrow that at times almost came close to the outpouring of grief after the death of the Princess of Wales. Young and old, they queued by the thousands to file past the Queen Mother's coffin at the lying-in-state in Westminster Hall. Orders went out to keep the building open day and night as people came from all over the United Kingdom to pay tribute. In chill April winds, some waited for up to eight hours, determined to play their part in a moment in history.

The Royal Family showed a new willingness to share their feelings with the public. They walked among the crowds, reminiscing about the Queen Mother and thanking people for coming. Prince Charles, who was devoted to his grandmother, made a moving televised tribute to her, saying:

She was the original life enhancer, whether publicly or privately, whoever she was with … At once indomitable, somehow timeless, able to span the generations, wise, loving, with an utterly irresistible mischievousness of spirit … She seemed gloriously unstoppable, and ever since I was a child, I adored her … She was quite simply the most magical grandmother you could possibly have.

On April 9, the day of the Queen Mother's funeral, a million people lined the route as her coffin was borne on a gun carriage to Westminster Abbey. The massed pipes and drums of thirteen regiments accompanied her, while the senior male members of the family, along with the Princess Royal, walked behind. It was a grand and sombre pageant, befitting a former Queen Consort, the last Empress of India.

Despite her double bereavement, the Queen decided that the Jubilee celebrations should go ahead as planned. On May 1, she and the Duke set off on a tour of seventy towns and cities throughout the UK. It took them from the south-west of England up to the Highlands and islands of Scotland, as well as to Wales and Northern Ireland. The Queen said it was her wish to thank people for their loyalty and support over the fifty years of her reign.

It was a test of endurance for a couple now well into old age but they were rewarded with a welcome far more enthusiastic than many people had expected. Time and again, crowds up to twenty thousand strong waited to see them. Every region they visited made it an excuse for a party; there was street theatre and music wherever they went.

The highlight of those three months of travelling was the main Jubilee weekend: a four-

day festival at the beginning of June. They were four days that proved the sceptics comprehensively wrong; four days when a million people in London and many more around the country joined in a party that few of them will ever forget.

The focus of the celebrations in the capital was Buckingham Palace, which – in a bold initiative organized by the BBC – was transformed for two evenings into a magnificent concert arena. Twelve thousand people, randomly drawn from a ballot, were invited into the Queen's back garden each evening. On the Palace lawns they were given champagne hampers to enjoy a picnic before taking their seats for the concert. Most couldn't believe their luck. The first evening was classical: serene and

elegant in keeping with the surroundings. The second was pop: raucous and outrageous, as the Palace rock'n'rolled. The concerts were relayed on giant screens to the huge crowds outside. Everyone, it seemed, wanted to join in. Afterwards the Queen lit the last in a chain of almost two thousand beacons and, as its flames shot skywards outside the Palace, two-and-half tons of fireworks exploded into deafening action from the roof.

The final day of the festivities brought another million people onto the streets: this time to witness the pageantry of a great state occasion and a carnival staged by twenty thousand performers. For only the third time in her reign, the Queen rode in the Gold State Coach – used at her coronation and her Silver Jubilee. It took her to St Paul's Cathedral for a service of thanksgiving. At a Guildhall lunch that followed, she gave her view of the Jubilee:

> Gratitude, respect and pride. These words sum up how I feel about the people of this country and the Commonwealth, and what this Golden Jubilee means to me.

The Golden Jubilee had been an undisputed success. The monarchy was riding high and, in October, the Queen and Duke cemented that success with a final Jubilee tour: this time to Canada. It took them from the outer reaches of the Arctic Circle all the way to Vancouver: from coast to coast a round trip of ten thousand miles.

On their return, though, they found that a courtroom sensation was about to undo much of their good work of previous months. The trial of Paul Burrell – former butler to the Princess of Wales – turned out to be the most dramatic of recent times. He was accused of stealing more than three hundred items belonging to Diana, Prince Charles and Prince William. In the third week of the hearing, however, a sudden intervention by the Queen halted the proceedings. She revealed to Prince Charles that, five years earlier, Mr Burrell had told her that he was storing some of the late Princess's papers for safe-keeping. When this information was passed on to the judge, the Old Bailey trial collapsed in a blaze of publicity. The Queen, the media trumpeted, must be either stupid or senile.

When Mr Burrell then sold his story to the *Daily Mirror*, a war of words erupted among the tabloids. Each day brought more salacious allegations – about the butler, about the Princess and about the Royal Family. It was a PR disaster; the debate about the value of a monarchy in modern-day society was re-ignited. The euphoria of the Jubilee seemed but a distant memory.

The Queen, though, has learned through bitter experience to take a long-term view of public opinion. She was said to be "philosophical" about this latest barrage of criticism. It did not, however, go unnoticed that she shed a tear at a memorial service for the war dead – her thoughts perhaps turning not only to their sacrifice but also to her own troubles and bereavements in what had started out as a year of celebration.

There's no doubt that the sorry saga of the Burrell trial – and the collapse of a second butler's trial a few weeks later – tarnished the Golden Jubilee Year. However, 2002 will almost certainly be remembered more for the goodwill generated in the earlier months than for the mistakes made at the end.

It remains true that, in fifty years, the Queen has rarely set a foot wrong and has accumulated a vast experience of world affairs. Many of the ten British Prime Ministers of her reign have spoken of the wise head she brings to national and international problems. She remains passionate about the Commonwealth and has earned the respect of its family of nations. Here at home, even republicans measure the start of any Presidency – if one were to come about – only from the end of her reign. She has struggled to bring herself into the twenty-first century; she's learned to surf the Internet and has acquired a mobile phone. At heart, however, she is still a country woman, never happier than when she is with her horses or at the races.

The world has changed radically in the half century since she came to the throne and the public can be fickle. The age of deference has passed – quite rightly. The Queen is aware that loyalty and affection cannot be taken for granted.

As a royal correspondent I held out the hope that to mark the Golden Jubilee milestone of her reign the Queen might have risked one more foray into the world of television. An interview in which we could hear her perspective on all that has happened and discover how she views the future of the institution to which she has dedicated her life would, indeed, have made the year truly special. It was, though, a forlorn hope. There is no doubt that the Queen believes that one of her greatest strengths is that she remains, for most of us, something of an enigma. And in that, she may well be right.

February 15, 2002: the saddest start to her Jubilee Year. The Queen attends the funeral of her only sister, Princess Margaret, with the Princess's daughter, Lady Sarah Chatto, at her side. Leading the mourners is the Princess's son, Viscount Linley, and his wife Serena.

The work of monarchy goes on. The Queen is given a warm and sympathetic welcome in Montego Bay, Jamaica, during an official visit just a few days after Princess Margaret's funeral.

April 9, 2002: the Royal Family, and the nation, mourn Queen Elizabeth the Queen Mother. Her funeral was held amid great pageantry at Westminster Abbey.

Not just a monarch that day, but a daughter bereft at the loss of her mother, the Queen takes a last look as Queen Elizabeth's coffin is borne on high.

A rare glimpse of the private woman, giving way to her grief for a brief moment.

On her Jubilee tour of the UK the Queen
went on more than fifty walkabouts in
seventy towns and cities – and was given
more bouquets than anyone could count.

Despite the gruelling schedule –
and her seventy-six years – the
Queen seemed genuinely to enjoy
her travels around her Kingdom.

Come rain or shine, the show goes on. The Queen and Duke shrug off the bad weather at the launch of Music Live in Slough.

June 1: a Royal Box in her own backyard. The Queen acknowledges the cheers of the twelve thousand guests who were invited to share the Prom at the Palace at the start of the Golden Jubilee festivities in June.

Betty meets Becks: at the opening of the Commonwealth Games in Manchester, the Queen is introduced to soccer hero David Beckham.

June 3: one of the family at last! After years of being frozen out, Camilla Parker Bowles joins the Queen and other members of the Royal Family for the Jubilee concerts.

Their relationship has not always been easy but, after the Party at the Palace, Prince Charles sealed a glowing tribute to his mother with a kiss.

Laser beams and fireworks light up the night sky as the Palace rock'n'rolled and a million people joined in.

June 4: after the raucous party, a return to pageantry as the Queen made her way from the Palace in the Gold State Coach, watched by another million.

It was the biggest street party in the world. Twenty thousand performers took part in a carnival down the Mall. It lasted more than three hours and drew another million people to the Palace to watch.

The parade had something for everyone: even the Hell's Angels joined in on their motorbikes – to the obvious amusement of the Queen and Duke, with Prince Charles and the Countess of Wessex.

PREVIOUS PAGES: Who said no one would turn out? There wasn't an inch to be found in the Mall as the huge crowds joined in an uproarious rendition of Land of Hope and Glory.

From the Palace balcony it must have been a stupendous sight: a forest of flags, an ocean of humanity all cheering the Queen. She was heard to remark: "Is this really all for me?"

Home at last! The last official engagement of the UK Jubilee Tour: a garden party at Balmoral. The Queen was said to be very tired after her travels but elated by the welcome she'd been given. Ahead lay eight weeks of rest and recuperation.

November 7: tears at the end of a roller coaster of a
year. The Queen gives way to her emotions as she
takes her mother's place at the Field of Remembrance
at St Margaret's Church, Westminster.

CHRONOLOGY

1926–2002

1926–1951

April 21, 1926: Elizabeth Alexandra Mary, first child of the Duke and Duchess of York, is born at 27 Bruton Street, London.

August 21, 1930: Princess Margaret Rose is born at Glamis Castle, Scotland.

May 6, 1935: Elizabeth attends the Silver Jubilee Thanksgiving Service for her grandfather, George V.

January 20, 1936: George V dies and is succeeded by Edward VIII.

December 11, 1936: Edward VIII abdicates and is succeeded by the Duke of York, who takes name George VI; Elizabeth is now Heir Presumptive.

May 12, 1937: George VI and Queen Elizabeth are crowned in Westminster Abbey.

September 3, 1939: Britain declares war on Germany.

October 1940: Elizabeth makes her first radio broadcast.

April 1945: Elizabeth joins the Auxiliary Territorial Service.

May, 1945: Elizabeth, Margaret celebrate VE Day.

Summer 1946: Prince Philip of Greece proposes to Elizabeth; her parents ask them to wait.

February–April 1947: The Royal Family tours South Africa and other British colonies in the region. Four days before leaving South Africa, Elizabeth marks her twenty-first birthday with a radio broadcast to the British Commonwealth and Empire, dedicating herself to their service.

July 10, 1947: Elizabeth's engagement to Lieutenant Philip Mountbatten announced.

November 20, 1947: Elizabeth and Philip marry in Westminster Abbey.

November 14, 1948: Elizabeth and Philip's first child, Charles Philip Arthur George, is born at Buckingham Palace.

June 1949: Elizabeth takes the salute in place of her ailing father at the Trooping the Colour ceremony.

December 1949: Elizabeth joins her husband in Malta, where he is on active service with the Royal Navy.

August 15, 1950: Princess Anne Elizabeth Alice is Louise born.

October 1951: Elizabeth and Philip become the first members of the Royal Family to fly the Atlantic, going to Canada for an official visit.

1952

January 31: Elizabeth and Philip leave London on the first leg of a major tour of the South Pacific, flying to Kenya.

February 6: George VI dies in his sleep at Sandringham. Elizabeth accedes to the throne.

February 7: Elizabeth and Philip return to London.

February 8: The Queen attends the formal meeting of her Accession Council at St James' Palace.

February 11: George VI's coffin is brought to London for three days of lying-in-state at Westminster Hall.

February 15: George VI's funeral is held at St. George's Chapel, Windsor.

June: The Queen takes the salute at the first Trooping the Colour of her reign.

November: The Queen attends the first State Opening of Parliament of her reign.

December 25: The Queen makes her first Christmas broadcast.

1953

February: The Queen visits flooded areas in England.

March: Marshal Tito of Yugoslavia lunches with the Queen.

March 24: Queen Mary dies at Marlborough House, aged eighty-five.

May 29: New Zealander Edmund Hillary and Sherpa Tensing Norgay reach the summit of Mount Everest; the news of this symbolic triumph of Empire reaches London in time to cheer the waiting crowds on the morning of the Coronation.

June 2: The Coronation of Queen Elizabeth II at Westminster Abbey. For the first time, much of the ceremony is televised.

November 24: The Queen and Duke of Edinburgh begin a five-and-a-half month Commonwealth tour.

1954

January: Royal tour continues in New Zealand, where the Queen opens Parliament.

February: The royal tour moves on to Australia, where the Queen opens Parliament in Canberra.

April: The royal tour moves on to Ceylon (now Sri Lanka) and Uganda.

May: The Queen and the Duke of Edinburgh are reunited with their two children in Libya, and take possession of the new Royal Yacht *Britannia*, on which they return to England via Malta and Gibraltar.

1955

April 5: Churchill resigns; Sir Anthony Eden becomes Prime Minister in his place.

July: The Queen receives Indian Prime Minister Pandit Nehru at Windsor.

October 31: After nearly two years of rumour and counter-rumour, Princess Margaret announces that she will not marry Group Captain Peter Townsend.

1956

January–February: The Queen and Duke of Edinburgh undertake a three-week tour of Nigeria.

April: The new Soviet leaders, Nikita Khrushchev and Nikolai Bulganin, visit the Queen at Windsor Castle.

October. 29: After a secret deal between Britain, France and Israel, about which the Queen is not informed, Israeli troops invade Egypt.

October 31: Anglo–French forces bomb Egyptian military targets, including airfields.

November 6: A Suez Canal Zone ceasefire begins.

1957

January 9: Anthony Eden resigns as Prime Minister.

January 10: The Queen asks Harold Macmillan to form new government.

January 28: Prince Charles begins his education at a London day school, Hill House; he is the first heir to the throne to be educated outside the palace.

February 22: Amid stories of a rift between the couple, the Queen announces that her husband is from now on to be known as Prince Philip, Duke of Edinburgh.

August: Lord Altrincham's famous article on the future of the Monarchy, including direct criticism of the Queen, is published in the *National and English Review.*

September: Prince Charles starts boarding school – Cheam Preparatory School in Hampshire.

October 12: The Queen and Prince Philip fly to Ottawa for a North American tour, during which they meet US President Dwight D. Eisenhower.

December 25: The Queen's Christmas broadcast is televised for the first time.

1958

June: The Queen goes into a coal mine for first time, wearing white overalls, boots and a helmet.

July: The names of the first life peers (barons and baronesses) are announced.

July: The Queen announces at the Empire and Commonwealth Games in Cardiff that she is to create Charles, Prince of Wales.

October: The State Opening of Parliament is televised for first time.

1959

June: Queen and Prince Philip begin six-week tour of Canada, during which the Queen and President Eisenhower open the St Lawrence Seaway and the Queen visits Chicago.

August: President and Mrs Eisenhower visit the Queen at Balmoral.

October: A General Election is held, Harold Macmillan remains Prime Minister.

1960

February 8: The Queen announces that she wishes her descendents to bear the name Mountbatten–Windsor.

February 19: The Queen gives birth to Prince Andrew Albert Christian Edward at Buckingham Palace.

February 26: The engagement is announced of Princess Margaret to Anthony Armstrong-Jones.

April: President de Gaulle of France makes a three-day state visit to Britain.

May 6: Princess Margaret marries Anthony Armstrong-Jones at Westminster Abbey.

1961

May: The Queen and Prince Philip visit Italy; they are received by Pope John XIII in the Vatican.

June: The Queen and Prince Philip receive President Kennedy and his wife, Jacqueline, at Buckingham Palace.

August: The Queen and Prince Philip visit Northern Ireland.

1962

May: Prince Charles becomes a pupil at Gordonstoun School in Scotland.

1963

January: The Queen and Prince Philip visit Canada.

February: The Queen and Prince Philip visit Fiji, New Zealand and Australia.

October 18: Harold Macmillan resigns as Prime Minister. Sir Alec Douglas-Home becomes Prime Minister.

December: The Queen attends memorial services for President Kennedy, who had been assassinated in November.

1964

March 10: The Queen gives birth to her fourth child, Prince Edward Antony Richard Louis.

October: Harold Wilson, leader of the Labour Party, becomes Prime Minister

October: The Queen and Prince Philip visit Canada.

1965

January 24: Sir Winston Churchill dies and, at the Queen's instigation, is given a state funeral, which she attends.

February: The Queen pays a state visit to Ethiopia and the Sudan.

March 15: The Queen visits the Duke of Windsor in a London hospital.

May: The twentieth anniversary of the ending of the Second World War is marked by Queen paying state visit to West Germany.

November 11: Rhodesia unilaterally declares independence from Britain; British government declares the move illegal and imposes sanctions on Rhodesia.

1966

January: Prince of Wales leaves Britain to spend six months at Timbertop, the country wing of Geelong Grammar School in Australia.

February: The Queen and Prince Philip undertake a month-long tour of the Caribbean.

May: Seamen's Strike causes the Queen to sign a proclamation of emergency.

June 11: Commonwealth Day observed for the first time.

July: The Queen presents the World Cup trophy to the England football team.

October: The Queen and Prince Philip visit Aberfan after the slag heap disaster that killed 144 people, mainly children.

1967

June 7: The Queen unveils a plaque to Queen Mary at Marlborough House; Duke and Duchess of Windsor attend the ceremony.

July 7: The Queen knights round-the-world yachtsman, Francis Chichester, at a public ceremony at Greenwich.

July: The Queen and Prince Philip visit Expo 67 in Canada.

September: The Queen launches the *QE2* in Glasgow.

1968

November: The Queen pays state visits to Peru and Chile and visits Senegal.

1969

February: The Queen entertains US President Richard M Nixon.

June: Television documentary, *Royal Family*, screened to widespread acclaim.

July 1: Investiture of Prince Charles as Prince of Wales at Caernarvon Castle.

October: The Queen receives Apollo 11 astronauts at Buckingham Palace.

November 14: Prince of Wales celebrates his twenty-first birthday.

1970

March: The Queen, Prince Philip, Prince of Wales and Princess Anne visit Fiji, Tonga, New Zealand and Australia.

June 18: Edward Heath becomes Prime Minister.

July: The Queen, Prince Philip, Prince of Wales and Princess Anne visit Canada.

July: The Queen attends the Commonwealth Games in Edinburgh.

1971

May: The Queen asks for a revision of the Civil List.

August 15: Princess Anne celebrates her twenty-first birthday on board *Britannia*.

October: State visit of Emperor Hirohito and the Empress of Japan to the UK.

November: President Tito of Yugoslavia lunches with the Queen.

December 2: The Select Committee on the Civil List report is delivered to the House of Commons, recommending an income rise.

1972

January: The Queen pays a state visit to Thailand and tours South East Asia and the Indian Ocean

May 18: The Queen starts a five-day state visit to France, during which she visits her uncle, the Duke of Windsor, at his Paris home.

May 28: The Duke of Windsor dies of cancer in Paris. His body is flown back to England and his coffin displayed for two days at St. George's Chapel, Windsor. The Duchess of Windsor stays at Buckingham Palace for the funeral.

November 20: The Queen and Prince Philip celebrate their silver wedding anniversary.

1973

January 1: United Kingdom becomes a member of the EEC; the Queen attends a gala marking the occasion.

May 30: The engagement of Princess Anne to Captain Mark Phillips is announced.

July: The Queen, accompanied by Prince Philip, attends the Commonwealth Heads of Government meeting in Canada.

October: The Queen opens the Sydney Opera House in Australia.

November 14: Princess Anne and Mark Phillips are married in Westminster Abbey.

1974

January: The Queen and Prince Philip leave for a long tour of the South Pacific and Australasia, including the Cook Islands, New Zealand, Norfolk Island, the New Hebrides, British Solomon Islands, Papua New Guinea and Australia. Opens the Commonwealth Games in Christchurch, New Zealand.

March: The Queen pays a state visit to Indonesia.

March 20: Princess Anne escapes a kidnap attempt in the Mall in London.

October: Prime Minister Harold Wilson calls a General Election, at which he secures a clear majority.

1975

February: The Queen and Prince Philip pay a state visit to Mexico.

May: The Queen and Prince Philip pay a state visit to Japan.

1976

March 16: Princess Margaret and Lord Snowdon announce their separation.

March 16: Harold Wilson resigns. His successor is James Callaghan.

April 21: The Queen celebrates her fiftieth birthday at Windsor.

July: The Queen and Prince Philip pay a state visit to the US, the year of the country's Bicentennial.

July: The Queen opens the twenty first Olympic Games in Montreal, Canada, in which Princess Anne is a competitor.

1977

February: The Queen and the Royal Family attend morning service at St. George's Chapel, Windsor, to mark the start of her Silver Jubilee year.

February–March: The Queen and Prince Philip visit Western Samoa, Tonga, Fiji, New Zealand, Australia and Papua New Guinea.

June: Silver Jubilee celebrations in Britain: events include a countrywide chain of bonfires, Thanksgiving Service in St. Paul's Cathedral, Guildhall lunch, an extensive UK tour by the Queen and Prince Philip, and a Silver Jubilee review of the Fleet at Spithead, Portsmouth.

July: The Queen presents the Wimbledon Ladies Singles trophy to Virginia Wade.

October: The Queen and Prince Philip visit Canada and the Caribbean.

November 15: Princess Anne gives birth to her first child, Peter.

1978

May: It is announced that Princess Margaret and Lord Snowdon will divorce.

Summer: The Queen and Prince Philip make a state visit to West Germany, during which they fly to Berlin, still in East Germany and surrounded by the Wall.

August: The Queen opens the Commonwealth Games in Edmonton, Canada.

1979

February: The Queen and Prince Philip make a three-week visit to several Gulf States.

May: Margaret Thatcher becomes the UK's first female prime minister.

July: The Queen, Prince Philip and Prince Andrew tour Tanzania, Malawi, Botswana and Zambia.

August 27: Earl Mountbatten of Burma assassinated by the IRA in Eire.

September 5: State funeral of Lord Mountbatten at Westminster Abbey.

November: The Queen's art adviser, Sir Anthony Blunt, is named as a Soviet spy.

1980

May: The Queen and Prince Philip visit Australia. They also conduct a state visit to Switzerland, the first by a reigning British monarch that century.

July 15: Thanksgiving service at St. Paul's Cathedral for the Queen Mother's eightieth birthday.

August 4: The Queen Mother's eightieth birthday.

October: The Queen and Prince Philip make state visit to Italy, including the Vatican; they also visit Tunisia, Algeria and Morocco.

1981

February 24: The engagement of the Prince of Wales to Lady Diana Spencer is announced.

May 15: Princess Anne gives birth to her second child, Zara.

June 6: Blank shots fired at the Queen as she rides to the Trooping the Colour ceremony.

July 29: The Prince of Wales and Lady Diana Spencer marry in St. Paul's Cathedral.

September–October: The Queen and Prince Philip visit Australia, New Zealand and Sri Lanka.

1982

February 6: The thirtieth anniversary of the Queen's Accession is celebrated.

April: Argentina invades the Falkland Islands.

June: President Reagan visits the UK and is entertained at Windsor.

June 21: Birth of Prince William of Wales.

July 9: The Queen wakes at Buckingham Palace to find an intruder, Michael Fagan, sitting on her bed.

July: A troop of the Queen's personal guards from the Blues and Royals blown up by IRA bomb in Hyde Park; band of the Royal Green Jackets bombed by IRA in Regent's Park.

September 17: The Queen welcomes Prince Andrew and other troops back from the Falklands.

October: The Queen visits Australia, Papua New Guinea, Solomon Islands, Nauru, Kiribati, Tuvalu and Fiji.

1983

February: The Queen and Prince Philip visit Jamaica, Cayman Islands, Mexico, USA and Canada.

March: The Queen and Prince Philip visit California, President Reagan's home state, staying at his ranch.

October: The Queen angered by American invasion of Grenada, a Commonwealth country of which she is head of state.

November: The Queen and Prince Philip visit Kenya, Bangladesh and India. In India, the Queen meets Mother Teresa in Calcutta.

1984

June: The Queen leads British participation in the fortieth anniversary commemoration of D-Day.

September–October: The Queen and Prince Philip visit Canada.

Sept 15: Prince Henry (Harry) is born.

October 12: IRA explodes a bomb at the Grand Hotel in Brighton during the Conservative Party Conference.

November: President Mitterand of France makes state visit to UK.

1985

February: The Queen visits *The Times* newspaper on its two hundredth anniversary.

March: The Queen and Prince Philip visit Portugal.

1986

February: The Queen and Prince Philip visit Nepal; also Australia and New Zealand.

April 21: Six thousand children gather at Buckingham Palace to sing "Happy Birthday" to the Queen on her sixtieth birthday.

July 23: Prince Andrew, now Duke of York, marries Sarah Ferguson in Wesminster Abbey.

October: The Queen and Prince Philip make state visit to China.

1987

May: The Queen and Prince Philip visit Germany,

June 19: Prince Edward's charity television spectacular, *It's A Royal Knock-Out*, is screened.

October: The Queen and Prince Philip visit Canada.

1988

April: The Queen and Prince Philip visit Australia.

July: The Queen and Prince Philip visit the Netherlands.

August 8: Duke and Duchess of York's first child, Princess Beatrice, is born.

October: The Queen and Prince Philip visit Spain.

1989

March: The Queen and Prince Philip visit Barbados.

April: President Mikhail Gorbachev of the USSR makes state visit to Britain, staying at Windsor.

October: The separation of Princess Anne and Mark Phillips is announced.

October: The Queen and Prince Philip visit Singapore and Malaysia.

1990

February: The Queen and Prince Philip make visits to New Zealand, Australia and Canada.

March 23: Princess Eugenie, second child of Duke and Duchess of York, is born.

June: The Queen and Prince Philip visit Iceland.

August: Iraq invades Kuwait.

November: Margaret Thatcher is ousted as leader of the Conservative Party and Prime Minister John Major wins resulting leadership contest and becomes Prime Minister.

1991

January: US, British and Saudi forces begin massive attack on Iraqis in Kuwait.

April: Lech Walesa, President of Poland, pays a state visit to the UK.

May: The Queen and Prince Philip visit Washington, the Queen becoming the first British Head of State to address a joint meeting of Congress. They also visit Florida and Texas.

October: The Queen and Prince Philip visit Namibia and Zimbabwe.

1992

February 6: The fortieth anniversary of the Queen's Accession is celebrated.

February: The Queen and Prince Philip visit Australia for the one hundred and fiftieth anniversary of Sydney City Council.

March: The separation of the Duke and Duchess of York is announced.

April: Princess Anne and Mark Phillips are divorced.

June: *Diana: Her True Story*, by Andrew Morton, is published.

November 20: Windsor Castle is seriously damaged by fire.

November 24: The Queen's anniversary lunch at Guildhall, during which she makes her "*annus horribilis*" speech.

November 26: It is announced that the Queen will pay income tax from now on.

December 9: The separation of the Prince and Princess of Wales is announced.

December: The royal yacht *Britannia* is decommissioned.

December 12: Princess Anne marries Tim Laurence.

December: *Sun* newspaper publishes text of Queen's Christmas message in advance, leaving her very distressed. She sues for breach of copyright.

1993

May: The Queen and Prince Philip visit Hungary.

September: Bobo MacDonald, the Queen's former nursemaid and dresser for sixty-seven years, dies.

October: The Queen and Prince Philip visit Cyprus.

1994

February–March: The Queen and Prince Philip tour the Caribbean.

June: Screening of Jonathan Dimbleby's television documentary about Prince Charles.

August: The Queen and Prince Philip visit Canada.

October: The Queen and Prince Philip undertake state visit to Russia.

1995

March: The Queen and Prince Philip visit South Africa, meeting President Nelson Mandela.

May: The Queen leads the nation in commemorating the fiftieth anniversary of VE Day.

October: The Queen and Prince Philip visit New Zealand.

November 20: Princess Diana gives her notorious interview to the BBC *Panorama* program.

December: The Queen writes to Charles and Diana, urging them to divorce.

1996

March: The Queen and the Princess Royal visit Dunblane, after the massacre at a school there.

March: The Queen and Prince Philip visit Poland and the Czech Republic.

April: The Duke and Duchess of York divorce.

August: The Prince and Princess of Wales divorce.

October: The Queen and Prince Philip visit Thailand.

1997

May 1: Tony Blair becomes Prime Minister.

June: The Queen and Prince Philip visit Canada.

July 1: Hong Kong returned to Chinese rule.

August 31: Princess Diana dies in a car crash in Paris.

September 6: Princes Diana's funeral takes place in London.

October: The Queen and Prince Philip undertake a tour of Pakistan and India.

November 20: The Queen and Prince Philip celebrate their golden wedding anniversary.

INDEX

ACKNOWLEDGEMENTS

The publishers would like to thank the following sources for their kind permission to reproduce the pictures in this book:
6 Corbis/Bettmann 12 Corbis/ EO Hoppe 13 b Corbis/Hulton Deutsch 13 Popperfoto 14 Corbis /Hulton Deutsch 15 Hulton/Archive/Studio Lisa 16 Corbis 16 t Popperfoto 17 Topham/Press Association 18 Corbis /Bettmann 19 t Corbis/Hulton Deutsch 19 b Topham/Press Association 20 Corbis/Hulton Deutsch 23 t Popperfoto 23 b Popperfoto 24 Popperfoto 25 Popperfoto 26 t Hulton/Archive/Studio Lisa 26 b Hulton/Archive/Studio Lisa 27 Hulton/Archive 28 t Corbis/Hulton Deutsch 28 Topham 29 Corbis/HultonDeutsch 30 t Hulton/Archive 30 b PA Photos 31 Popperfoto 32 Topham 34 Topham 36 b Hulton/Archive 36 t Popperfoto 37 Topham 38 t Corbis/Hulton Deutsch 38 b Topham 39 Camera Press/James Reid 40 Topham 41 Corbis 42/43 Topham 44 Corbis/Hulton Deutsch 45 Popperfoto 46 b Topham 46 t Topham 47 Popperfoto 48/49 Topham 50 Hulton/Archive 51 t Corbis/Bettmann 51 b Topham 52 Camera Press/Cecil Beaton 53 Corbis /Bettmann 54 b Hulton/Archive 54 t Popperfoto 55 Hulton/Archive 56 Hulton/Archive 57 Topham 58 Hulton/Archive 59 Hulton/Archive 60 Hulton/Archive 61 Popperfoto 62 Topham 63 Hutlon Getty 64 Popperfoto 67 Hulton/Archive 68 Hulton/Archive 69 Hulton/Archive 70 Topham 71 b Camera Press/Cecil Beaton 71 t Popperfoto 72 Hulton 73 t Hulton/Archive 73 b Popperfoto 74/75 Hulton/Archive 76 t Hulton/Archive 76 b Hulton/Archive 77 Hulton/Archive 78 b Hulton/Archive 78 t Popperfoto 79 t Hulton/Archive 79 b Hulton/Archive 80 Corbis/Hulton Deutsch 81 b Popperfoto 81 t Popperfoto 82/83 PA Photos 84 PA Photos 85 Topham 86 Hulton/Archive 87 Hulton/Archive 88 Topham 89 t Hulton/Archive 89 b Hulton/Archive 90 Hulton/Archive 91 Hulton/Archive 92 Popperfoto 93 b Hulton/Archive 93 t Popperfoto 94 Corbis/Hulton Deutsch 96 Topham/Press Association 98 Hulton/Archive 99 t Camera Press/Patrick Lichfield 99 b Hulton/Archive 100b Corbis/Bettmann 100 t Popperfoto 101 Popperfoto 102 b Hulton/Archive 102 t Topham 103 Hulton/Archive 104/105 Hulton/Archive 106/107 PA Photos 107 b Corbis/HultonDeutsch 108 t Hulton/Archive 108 b Hulton/Archive 109 t Hulton/Archive 109 b Hulton/Archive 110 t Hulton/Archive 110 b Topham 111 t Hulton/Archive 111 b Topham/Press Association 112 Topham/Press Association 113 t Camera Press/PatrickLichfield 113 b Popperfoto 114 Topham 116 Topham 118 t Corbis 118 b Hulton/Archive 119 t Photo La Presse/Ron Poling b Corbis/Bettmann 120 Corbis/Hulton Deutsch 121 t Corbis/Bettmann 121b Hulton/Archive 122b Topham 122 t Topham/Associated Press 123 Corbis/Hulton Deutsch 124 Corbis/Hulton Deutsch 125 Topham 126 b Hulton/Archive 126 t Hulton/Archive 127 Topham 128/129 Popperfoto 130 Popperfoto 130 b Topham 130 t Topham/AP 131 Topham /Upp 136 Topham/Press Association 137 b PA Photos 137 t Topham 138 t PA 138 b PA 139 t Popperfoto 139 b Topham 140 t PA 140 b Popperfoto 141 t PA/John Stillwell 141 b Tim Graham 142/143 Tim Graham 144 PA 145 Topham 145 t Topham/Press Association 146 b PA/John Stillwell 146 t Topham 147 b Topham/Press Association 147 t Popperfoto/Adam Butler/Reuters 148 t PA/Fiona Hanson 148 b Topham 149 Popperfoto 150 b PA/William Conran 150 t Popperfoto 151 t PA 151b Popperfoto 152 b PA/Tony Harris 152 t Tim Graham 153 Popperfoto/Reuters/Kieran Doherty 154-155 Press Association, 158 PA, 160, PA, 161 Getty Images, 162 PA, 163 Rex (t), Corbis (b), 164, Corbis (tr), Rex (tl, bl, br), 165 Rex, 166 Corbis (b), Rex (t), 167 Rex (t), PA (b). 168-9 Corbis, 170 Rex (t), Corbis (b), 171 Corbis/Tim Graham
Every effort has been made to acknowledge correctly and contact the source and/or copyright holder of each picture, and Carlton Books Limited apologises for any unintentional errors or omissions which will be corrected in future editions of this book.